Philip J. Hermann is Chairman of the Board of the Lawyer-to-Lawyer Consultation Panel and has held such positions of authority as Chairman of the Federal Court Committee, Associate Editor of The *Forum,* and serving as member of the House of Delegates and Judicial Administration and Legal Reform Committee.

DO YOU NEED A Lawyer?

A SPECTRUM BOOK

PRENTICE-HALL, INC., Englewood Cliffs, N.J. 07632

Library of Congress Cataloging in Publication Data

Hermann, Philip J
Do you need a lawyer?

(A Spectrum Book)
Includes index.
1. Attorney and client—United States.
2. Pro se representation—United States.
3. Actions and defenses—United States.   4. Law—
United States—popular works.   I. Title.
KF311.H47   349.73   80-10999
ISBN 0-13-216721-2
ISBN 0-13-216713-1 pbk.

Cover design by IRA SHAPIRO
Interior design and editorial supervision by Shirley Covington and Chris Wolf
Manufacturing buyer: Barbara A. Frick

A SPECTRUM BOOK

10 9 8 7 6 5 4 3 2 1

Printed in the United States of America

PRENTICE-HALL INTERNATIONAL, INC., *London*
PRENTICE-HALL OF AUSTRALIA PTY. LIMITED, *Sydney*
PRENTICE-HALL OF CANADA, LTD., *Toronto*
PRENTICE-HALL OF INDIA PRIVATE LIMITED, *New Delhi*
PRENTICE-HALL OF JAPAN, INC., *Tokyo*
PRENTICE-HALL OF SOUTHEAST ASIA PTE. LTD., *Singapore*
WHITEHALL BOOKS LIMITED, *Wellington, New Zealand*

Table of Contents

Preface

How This Book Came into Being

The need was apparent. The public knew little or nothing about lawyers and the legal profession. What they thought they knew was often wrong. Most important, many failed to avail themselves of needed legal services, often with disastrous consequences.

The leaders of the legal profession have been aware of the situation for a long time and are uneasy about it. The facts show that information is needed by the public. But is it possible to put the necessary information into the hands of the people who need lawyers?

Legal societies and bar organizations studied the problem. The American Bar Association appointed a special committee to survey the legal needs of the public and came up with the conclusion that the middle 70% of the population was not being reached or adequately served by the legal profession. They discovered that a major problem was that the public didn't know how to locate suitable lawyers. Eighty-two % of nonusers agreed that a lot of people do not go to lawyers because they have no way of knowing which lawyer is competent to handle their particular problem.

It became obvious that a book was necessary—a how-to-do-it book on selecting a lawyer and hiring him, containing basic information about the profession, the courts, how a lawyer works, how he charges, how he can help, what you should do before you consult with him, what questions to ask, and. . . .

This is the book. We hope it helps you solve your legal problems at the lowest possible cost.

How to Choose and Hire A Good Lawyer

1

What do you know about lawyers?

By popular belief, a lawyer might as well have horns and a tail. Many people look upon the legal profession with doubt and suspicion. Many firmly believe that lawyers charge outrageously, that they are a bunch of crooks, and that they should be consulted only as a last resort. The fact is that lawyers have to be more honest and ethical than any businessman you know. A businessman can get by with shady practices and sharp dealings, with anything short of actual violation of a law. A lawyer is bound by a code of ethics and by professional responsibility, and his fellow lawyers can have him thrown out of the profession for any professional or personal misconduct. Of course, we do have lawyers who are not honest and not ethical, but they are fewer in number than the public realizes. Further, in the case of dishonesty on the part of a lawyer that results in loss to the client, it is frequently taken care of by a "Lawyers Security Fund," which has been set up by bar associations for the protection of clients.

Concerning charges for services, they are generally surprisingly modest. The Special Survey of Legal Needs found that 15.3% of all persons who consult lawyers are charged no fee whatsoever. True, sometimes fees *were* substantial, often because of the client's own fault—misusing counsel or failing to consult counsel earlier. The fact is that the average lawyer earns only half as much as the average doctor—often only as much as a plumber. The fact is that most legal services prove to be worth many times their cost to the client. This book explains how lawyers charge and how you can hold those charges to a minimum.

Competence to handle a client's specific problem is the most important consideration in choosing a lawyer. How do you know if a lawyer is competent to handle your problem? This book will help you select a lawyer best suited to your needs.

The common beliefs about lawyers are wrong or grossly exaggerated. Yet ignorance about the legal profession persists. Many persons actually fear lawyers. As a result, most people will hire a lawyer only as a last resort, after the legal situation is thoroughly muddled. Tangled legal problems take the lawyer's time to unravel, and a lawyer must charge for his time. This is why, generally, the public believes that lawyers are expensive.

Legal problems don't have to be knotty. If you get legal advice at the right time, a lawyer can often solve problems easily. In fact, according to the findings of a special committee of the American Bar Association, *25% of legal matters are resolved at the consultation stage*—at the initial meeting with a lawyer.

YOU NEED TO KNOW CERTAIN THINGS

You will need legal services at some time in your life. Therefore, it is very important that you know how to find and hire a good lawyer. It is as important as securing a competent family doctor. Your financial condition, your future, your property, your person, even your life may depend on having a lawyer you can call on when needed.

At this point, what do you really know about lawyers?

Do you know how lawyers work for you, how they protect your property and personal rights?

Do you know how to discuss legal fees, and how you can save money on legal services?

Do you know how to get your legal work done at minimum cost or at no cost to you at all?

Do you know what legal matters you can handle yourself? and when you should go to a lawyer?

Do you know what to do if you're not satisfied with your lawyer?

This book covers each of these points and many more. It is designed to fill a long-standing need for practical information about the legal profession.

The single most important question this book answers is: *How can I select and hire a competent lawyer who is exactly right for my needs?*

Would you know how to find a competent lawyer to handle your problem? Probably not. This is no reflection on you. Most Americans are helpless when it comes to selecting a lawyer who best meets their needs. You will recall that the special committee of the American Bar Association that surveyed this problem reported that 82% of the people who do not consult lawyers fail to do so because they have no way of knowing which lawyers are competent to handle their legal problems.

How could it be otherwise? You must have information before you can make an intelligent decision. The public, up to this time, has been almost totally uninformed about the legal profession. This book is a first attempt to provide step-by-step, how-to-do-it instructions on how to choose a lawyer in an intelligent manner and how to employ the legal system to best advantage.

Our purpose is to give you the basic information you need to help you find a lawyer who is ''good''—that is, competent to solve your particular legal problem.

158 DIFFERENT VARIETIES

One reason that random choice of a lawyer is usually a poor choice is that you may pick a lawyer who knows nothing about the law and procedure necessary to effectively and efficiently solve your particular problem. There are *158 fields of law.* A good divorce lawyer may be helpless in a tax case. A real estate lawyer may know nothing about personal injury law. A good general practitioner may be lost in a complicated business matter.

One chapter deals with the technical differences in lawyers. There are more "specialties" in the legal field than there are in the medical field. You should know how the "specialties" in the legal profession can be useful to you. (Although the public — and even lawyers — loosely refers to lawyers who devote their attention to a certain field of law as "specialists," the profession officially reserves this term for lawyers who are "certified" in a particular field by the profession. This is covered in the chapter on the fields of law.)

Lawyers are people, too. They are as varied as your friends. Some are brighter than others. Some are hard workers. Some are lazy. Some know their field of law very well. Others just slide by at the expense of their clients. We will suggest ways to size up a lawyer and make sure he — or she — is right for you.

SAVING MONEY ON LEGAL SERVICES

The cost of legal services is generally less than you might expect. The initial consultation may cost you a fee, or it may cost nothing at all. Where legal costs become high, it is often because the client has misinformed or misused legal counsel, thus causing unnecessary expenses. Ways will be suggested to avoid unnecessary expenses.

We will tell you how to secure high-grade legal services at the lowest possible cost. Very frequently, legal services will not cost you anything. Legal costs may be paid by others, or the cost may be returned to you out of the recovery of money and property. In many types of legal actions the attorney will not charge you anything unless he collects money for you—a recovery of money for you either by settlement with other parties or through court action. In many situations the lawyer's advice and services can save you many times the fee charged. Consultation with a lawyer may cost you a few dollars but save you much hardship and grief. A lawyer can safeguard your rights and your person in ways that cannot be measured in terms of money.

When a person needlessly puts himself and his property in jeopardy, the legal problems can grow mountainous. Many persons will not see a lawyer at an early stage because they are afraid that legal consultation will be too costly. Small problems become great problems. Eventually, when a lawyer is finally brought into the case to clean up the mess, many services may be required, legal services that could have been avoided by an early consultation and the payment of a small fee. *We will tell you how to discuss the fee basis with a lawyer to minimize the cost or to sometimes shift it to someone else.*

IF YOU ARE DISSATISFIED

If you are not satisfied with the way your lawyer is conducting your legal matters, you should know your rights. Should you suffer a loss as the result of what you believe to be malpractice or dishonesty on the part of a lawyer, this book will tell you what you can do about it.

In short, we try to cover the basics you should know about the legal profession. The book is written in nontechnical language, so that it can be easily understood and useful to you, regardless of your knowledge.

It will help you select a lawyer or a law firm that is best suited for your needs—whether you are a working person or a large corporation, whether your problem is personal or a business matter, whether you have only an occasional need for legal services or a continuing need.

HOW TO USE THIS BOOK

This book will give you an insight into the legal profession. It deserves your careful attention and a complete reading, because it contains the background information you need to choose and use a lawyer to your greatest advantage.

The Table of Contents is a time-saver. Use it to select the chapters that apply directly to your immediate problem.

Do You Really Need A Lawyer?

2

Going to a lawyer for advice is very similar to going to a physician when you have pains. It's human to put off going as long as possible. When you finally have a pain that is bad enough to be frightening, you will go to a doctor. Usually the doctor will advise you that it is a minor problem and prescribe something to relieve your fears. The fee you pay gives you peace of mind. If your physician does discover a serious situation that threatens your health or your life, you may then take steps to avoid serious or fatal illness.

Legal situations can also threaten your person and your peace of mind. Someone may be trying to take away your legal rights or to take away the things you own. When your property or your rights are in danger and you don't know what to do about it, you will want to see a legal doctor for advice. (Most lawyers today are Juris Doctors!) If you have no legal problem or it is nothing serious, you will be as relieved as you are after going to a physician for a physical checkup. Your lawyer will advise you on what can be done about any situation involving law.

It is the lawyer's job to *protect* and *defend* your legal rights, and to *help you claim what is rightfully yours* under the law.

Just as only a doctor can tell you whether you really need a doctor, only a lawyer can tell you whether you really need a lawyer. No book can give you a complete answer to your question, "Do I need a lawyer?" We can, however, give you a number of tests and guidelines to help you decide whether or not you need a lawyer, and these will be explored in the next few pages.

IGNORING A LEGAL PROBLEM CAN BE COSTLY

Doing nothing when you suspect you have a legal problem can have unfortunate consequences. Studies show that millions of persons are taken advantage of by others; millions of persons lose valuable rights. Most persons do not know what their legal rights are; as a result, they do not take the necessary steps to avoid problems and pitfalls or to protect and enforce their rights. Government studies indicate that about half of the persons in the middle-income group do not obtain legal services when they need such services, primarily because they think they can't afford a lawyer. (The question of whether lawyers are affordable is discussed in the next section.)

The same studies point out that those who do consult lawyers have a great advantage over those who don't. Studies point out that wealthy persons in general have an unfair advantage over persons in the lower-income bracket: A chief reason is that they consult lawyers and freely avail themselves of legal services while lower-income persons do not. Wealthy persons protect and enforce their rights, and in so doing they often find themselves in a position of great advantage over those who don't. You can have the same advantages, or at least protect your person and property regardless of your economic position. How? By the judicious use of lawyers.

YOU NEED A LAWYER ...

1. Whenever You Suspect That You Have a Legal Problem That Substantially Affects Your Rights to the Things You Own, Your Personal Rights, or Your Future, You Need to Consult a Lawyer

When you believe that you have a legal problem that affects an important right to your property or to your person, you should consult a lawyer. A brief consultation costing a few dollars may save you a lot of grief and a lot of money. Such a consultation may even bring money to you. Your lawyer will inform you of your legal rights and help you resolve the legal problem if you have one.

Even if your lawyer tells you that you have no legal problem—that you have no legal claim against another person, that there can be no legal claim against you yourself, and that you haven't done anything that could put your person in jeopardy—you will still get an important dividend from the consultation. You will have peace of mind. You will no longer wonder whether you have allowed an important legal right to slip away from you. You will not have the worry of wondering if you may be prosecuted for doing something that might be illegal.

Legal consultation may prevent you from having legal problems in the future, and this can be most important to you. Perhaps you have been doing something in such a way as to cause great legal difficulties later. As a result of your lawyer's consultation, you will know where you stand; you may wish to discontinue doing the thing that can bring legal entanglements, or you may continue but go about it in a different way.

Freely consulting a lawyer whenever you suspect you may have a legal problem will cost you some consultation fees — perhaps even many of them. However, in the long run, you are certain to be money ahead. Wealthy persons, for example, know by experience that legal fees cost far less than legal difficulties. When you consider the financial problems that a lawyer helps to avoid and the savings realized by being able to protect and enforce rights and claims successfully, the liberal user of legal counsel reaps financial benefits many times the cost of the fees. Legal counsel warns persons away from doing things that might put their futures or their persons in jeopardy.

Whatever your financial status may be, your personal rights are just as important to you as they are to a multimillionaire. You will find it well worth while to consult a lawyer and avail yourself of legal counsel whenever you have good reason to believe that you have a substantial legal right that is threatened.

2. If the Other Person Is Represented by a Lawyer

Would you go into the prize ring against a professional boxer? Would you, a duffer at golf, play for high stakes against a pro on the tour? Of course you wouldn't. Yet every day, untrained persons try to compete against highly skilled professionals in the field of law.

If you try to deal directly with a lawyer who represents another person with an interest adverse to your own—then you need to be represented by a lawyer also. *Adverse interest* means any interest that differs in any respect from your interest, your wants and desires and rights. If there is any question about adverse interest, you should consult your own lawyer. Don't let the other person try to talk you out of getting your own lawyer.

It is actually safer to ask the other person's attorney about possible adverse interest. Ask him if his client's interests and your interests may be adverse to each other. If he tells you that adverse interest may be a possibility, then you need a lawyer. If he tells you that his client's interests and yours are not adverse, ask him to put it in writing. If he does not do so, you need your own lawyer. If there is any further doubt, you can give him one more test. Ask him whether he would consider also representing your interest. The Code of Professional Responsibility prevents a lawyer from representing conflicting interests, unless he does so with the permission of all concerned.

If you know that the person with whom you are dealing is being advised by a lawyer, you should consider having a lawyer advise you.

3. If What You Are Doing Involves a Lot of Money

Legal mistakes may be unpleasant to you, but they will not hurt you greatly if only a small amount of money is involved. However, if what you are doing involves the kind of money that would seriously affect or hurt you if it were lost, you need a lawyer.

If you are buying a home or a business, or if you are considering investing in a business (other than by the purchase of stocks or bonds listed on a stock exchange), you need a lawyer because of the amount of money involved. You must be sure that your rights are protected and that you do not jeopardize your future rights. In any transaction involving a large sum of money when procedures are outside your usual course of business or experience—at any time when you may not be aware of possible entanglements—you need a lawyer.

If you are involved with a government agency of any kind, in connection with your business or otherwise, in a way that involves substantial rights or money, and if you do not understand what it's all about, you need a lawyer. If you believe that you have not been dealt with fairly or properly by any government agency or business, in any matter that will substantially affect your person, property, business, job, or future, you need a lawyer.

4. If You Are Involved in Something That Can Seriously Affect Your Future

A friend may ask you a favor, and that favor could seriously jeopardize your financial future or your person. You would do well to consult an attorney to see what you may be letting yourself in for. For example, you may be asked to sign another person's promissory note, "as a formality." Your signature on such a note would make you a *guarantor,* which means that you guarantee payment if your friend doesn't pay. You may find yourself saddled with another person's debt. Your signature binds you, and it is worth a great deal of money to you. Whenever someone asks you to sign a document you do not understand or to do something you believe may have important consequences in your future, you would be wise to consult a lawyer.

5. If You Are Charged or Suspect That You May Be Charged With Any Crime That Could Result in a Jail Sentence or a Large Fine or Loss of Your Driving Privileges

Some people believe that if you are innocent you have nothing to worry about. This is not necessarily true. Simply being charged with a serious crime, even though the charge is dropped or you are found innocent, may mean that your future will be ruined. Many may hear that you have been charged, few of these may hear that the charges were dropped or that you were found innocent. Many people think that if you are charged, you must be guilty.

Accordingly, even if you merely hear a rumor that you are being investigated or that you may be charged with a crime, you will find it highly important to immediately consult a lawyer. Many people without benefit of counsel make statements —even *sign* statements —that give the impression of guilt when that is not the situation nor the impression that they wish to convey.

Many people plead guilty to crimes that they are not guilty of because they are assured or given the impression that the penalty will be a fine that may be less than the cost of a lawyer. Even if true, pleading guilty to something you didn't do because it is economically attractive may haunt you the rest of your life. Before you do anything like that, you would do well to consult a lawyer.

Similarly, people plead guilty to traffic offenses that they shouldn't plead guilty to. They do so because they believe the fines are less than the cost of a lawyer. They then find that they may be put in jail, they may have their license suspended, or their auto insurance rate may be affected. To make it worse, they may have had a legitimate defense; furthermore, the lawyer might actually have cost much less than they were led to believe.

Consultation with a lawyer is inexpensive. Before you make a move or make any change that could seriously affect your future, you will do well to see a lawyer.

A final word of advice: in any situation, someone may tell you, ''You don't need a lawyer.'' If you are told this, *be suspicious*. The adviser may be trying to take advantage of you. It is unfortunate today that many business people, some with professional and semiprofessional status, will try to discourage you from consulting a lawyer—even though it involves substantial amounts of money and may seriously affect your future.

One reason that sellers often try to discourage buyers from consulting lawyers is that the additional time required allows buyers to more fully consider whether the purchase is wise and they may decide to back out. We can understand why salesmen want you to sign on the dotted line without delay—otherwise, they might lose sales. As a buyer, however, it is to your advantage to think over your purchase and consult a lawyer, even though it means that you may change your mind—often for good reason. In a real estate transaction, for example, if you consult a lawyer he may find that you are overpaying for a given property or that it is in a bad location or that there are many other problems with which you may not wish to get involved.

Ironically, the same sellers who will try to discourage prospective customers from seeing lawyers will probably themselves not make purchases of consequence without having the entire matter reviewed by their lawyers.

Every day lawyers are called upon to try to get people out of agreements that they entered into without the services of a lawyer. Unfortunately, it may require far more legal services at greater cost to get you out of a bad agreement than it would have cost you to avoid the problem by timely consultation.

You Do Not Need a Lawyer For All Legal Matters

3

Just because the services of a lawyer are usually called for by most people in certain situations does not necessarily mean that you should call in a lawyer. There are three main considerations in deciding whether or not to retain a lawyer.

First, you may have unusual familiarity in a particular field. Because of your knowledge, you may be able to handle the matter as well or almost as well as a lawyer.

Second, it may be a matter in which you can do a fair job of representing yourself, and you desire to do so. It may be a matter where economic factors make the hiring of a lawyer ridiculous because of the small amount involved. Or it may be a matter that really does not have to be handled by a lawyer, although many people might ask a lawyer to handle it.

Third, you may be able to call in people from other professions or with other skills who can do a creditable job. Let's discuss some of these.

YOUR SPECIAL KNOWLEDGE

Perhaps you are so knowledgeable that you don't need a lawyer. For example, suppose you are a real estate investor buying and selling real estate with frequency. You know what to look for in the contracts offered you, and you may have a purchase agreement that you have used many times before. There is no reason that you can't continue to handle such matters.

However, *if it's complicated—you may need a lawyer!* When you get involved in a complicated real estate situation requiring a specially tailored contract, you will find it advantageous to have a lawyer review or draw these contracts for you. Indeed, most experienced real estate traders would not think of handling such matters without the services of a lawyer.

If you have never purchased real estate before or have done so only on occasion, you would be foolish to handle such a transaction without the services of a lawyer. Not only can a lawyer help safeguard your legal rights in perhaps the most important financial transaction that you will ever make but, more often than not, he can also save you many times his fee by helping you avoid items that can be costly to you.

For example, in many areas of the country, vacant lots accumulate unpaid taxes. When builders decide to build on such lots, they frequently will go to the taxing authorities and arrange to *respread* the delinquent taxes over a period of years — perhaps as long as 15 or 20 years. The taxing authorities often agree to such propositions because builders will then put homes on the subdivisions and they will gain in current taxes. The selling price is usually arranged on the theory that *some of the purchasers will have lawyers, in which case the purchase agreement will require that all taxes due, even though not currently payable, must be paid by the developer or seller.*

The seller frequently has two contracts; one that he will use when he knows that you are represented by a lawyer and the other for use when he knows that no lawyer is involved. The first will provide that the seller will pay all delinquent taxes, even though they're respread.

If the seller knows that you are not represented by an attorney and so are not likely to know about the tax jeopardy, the contract he gives you will be silent on the matter; it will only refer to taxes due and payable. The difference to you, the purchaser, can easily be several thousand dollars. This often accounts for the fact that two identical homes built at the same time will have vastly different tax bills.

Here is an example from my personal experience: A man came into my office very disturbed. He had purchased a home next to that of his brother. Although the two homes were similar, his tax bill was approximately twice as high as his brother's. He went to the county treasurer to get it straightened out, and the treasurer recommended he see a lawyer. When I observed that his brother must have had a lawyer, he quickly said: "And you know that lawyer charged him $100 and didn't do a damn thing for him." He proudly observed that he saved a $100 lawyer's fee by handling the purchase himself. But it cost this man several thousand dollars in tax respreads—thousands of dollars that another lawyer saved his brother for a $100 fee.

IS IT REALLY A LEGAL MATTER?

Some cases are not really legal matters, especially at an early stage. These can be handled by you until they become legal matters. For example, suppose you were injured in an automobile accident that resulted from the carelessness of another driver. The insurance adjuster may be perfectly willing to take care of your medical expenses, loss of wages, and to pay you an amount that you are satisfied with for your pain and suffering.

In such event you don't necessarily need a lawyer. Your neighbor may tell you that if you get a lawyer the insurance company will pay more money. This may be true. However, after you consider the money that you have lost in wages to attend to various legal processes that may be involved; out-of-pocket expenses for court reporters, photographs, and so forth; and the loss of use of money that you could have had in the bank drawing interest, you may find that you actually end up with less than you would have if you had accepted the insurance adjuster's offer.

On the other hand, if it appears to you that the adjuster is not being fair with you, then you should consult a lawyer—if for no other reason than to assure yourself that the adjuster *is* being fair. If not, you may need a lawyer who can effect an equitable settlement. Equitable settlement means *satisfactory to you.*

CAN SOME OTHER PROFESSIONAL DO AS WELL?

There are some matters handled by lawyers that could be handled just as well, or sometimes even better, by members of other professions or by people with other specialized knowledge. For example, suppose you have a problem preparing your U.S. income tax return. An accountant, certainly a certified public accountant, may be able to do as good a job as a lawyer. However, if you get involved in a matter that might involve a claim of fraud or large penalties against you, you need the services of a lawyer who is highly skilled in the field of income tax law.

In the following chapters you will be given practical advice on how you, yourself, can handle a number of situations that are commonly encountered. The focus will be on getting the best possible results without hiring a lawyer. The emphasis is on the psychology that gets results—the same kind of psychology that lawyers often use as leverage. No attempt will be made to inform you of all the law that may be applicable. The reason is that the laws are complex and vary from state to state and from city to city. (A book on law for laymen often provides you with only enough legal principles to get you into trouble!) The focus here is on the practical factors that will produce best results with a minimum of time and effort on your part.

How to Handle Common Legal Problems Yourself

4

Your legal rights are on the line every day. Your daily activities will involve you with others. You may be at fault. Others may try to take advantage of you. Everyday happenings will affect your rights.

—A traffic policeman alleges that you were speeding and gives you a ticket you feel you don't deserve.
—You sign an agreement to purchase some furniture, and it's not satisfactory.
—Your new car has to be towed in for the third time in the four months you've had it.
—You are passed over for promotion and believe that you have been discriminated against.
—Your golf ball slices into the next fairway and hits another golfer in the head.
—Your dog bites your new neighbor.

Events in day-to-day living that could become legal problems are almost endless. In the course of any year you will be confronted by situations that may cost you money, threaten you with going to jail, result in fines, or cause just plain aggravation.

How often have you wished that you could have a lawyer on retainer to assist you with your everyday problems? It's good to have a family lawyer, if only for name-dropping purposes— someone you can consult in a serious problem.

But most of the day-to-day problems do not justify the expense of hiring a lawyer. Most problems don't involve enough money to make it economic to have a lawyer working on them. So if your budget is slim, you will do as most persons do—simply take your lumps. What are some of these "lumps"?

— Even though you don't believe that you were speeding, you hope that the traffic judge will not suspend your license and take away your driving privileges or make you pay a large fine.
— Even though the furniture that was delivered to your home appears inferior to the furniture you saw in the showroom, and the store refuses to take it back, you pay for it.
— Even though your car continues to give you trouble and all the car dealer does is send you hefty repair bills, you simply pay.
— And you take out the frustration of not being promoted by fighting with your wife or yelling at the kids.

Like most people in this world, you allow yourself to be kicked around. But there's an alternative.

YOU CAN HANDLE PROBLEMS AS A LAWYER WOULD

You can learn a few principles of law and the way lawyers use leverage in handling problems that can bring surprisingly good results. Don't expect to be as good as a lawyer. And don't try to handle something complicated or something that obviously needs the experience and knowledge of a good lawyer. Other than that, if you follow these suggestions and do your homework, you will be surprised how often and how well you can solve the small problems that used to defeat you. You will find it downright fun to prevent others from taking unfair advantage of you. It will bolster your ego and restore your confidence in your ability to cope in our complex society. And it should save you money as it helps protect your rights.

Sometimes a simple maneuver will solve the problem. Sometimes it may require you to spend hours of your time doing legal homework. If your time is too valuable or you don't have it to spare, you may be better off simply dropping the matter. At any rate, you will know the alternatives and be in a position to decide your course of action. You may decide that it's better to pay the traffic fine or forget about getting an adjustment on the defective automobile. And if you find that your driving rights are in jeopardy or that you may face a jail term, you will decide to secure the services of a lawyer.

THE MAGIC WORDS THAT HELP YOU GET RESULTS

There are two words you can use that have a magical effect in problem situations. Those magic words are "My Lawyer. . . . " When you find yourself being pushed around, you will be surprised how quickly everything changes when you say, "Unless you take care of this, I will see my lawyer about it." You don't have to have a family lawyer, of course. But it is a lot more convincing if you *do* have a lawyer you can call.

The instant you say the magic words, the furniture store that has refused to take back the cheaper furniture will suddenly discover that a mistake has been made. The traffic policeman may let you off with a warning. They don't want to tangle with a lawyer. They feel that it's smarter to deal *fairly* with you than to have to deal with legal entanglements, a sharp lawyer, and the extra expense and time.

About the only time "I will see my lawyer about this" doesn't work is when you haven't been convincing enough. Use the name of your lawyer. It's believable and helpful to your cause if you say, "I will see my lawyer, Joseph Smith, about this." This is far more likely to produce good results. The person you are dealing with knows that you at least know the name of a lawyer. If he accepts it at face value, he will treat you as a person who cannot be shoved around easily (as most persons can be). It's handy to have a working relationship with a lawyer so you can convincingly drop his name. It's even more convincing if you ask to use the telephone so that you can call your lawyer, Joseph Smith, and if you have the number to call. Your would-be oppressor may decide to make it unnecessary for you to make the call.

THE IMPACT OF THREATENING TO SUE

What is even more frightening to persons who are not dealing fairly with you is the prospect of being sued. Saying "I will have my lawyer sue you" often sends chills down their backs. They not only face the prospect that it may cost them money to hire a lawyer to combat your lawyer, they also have to face the prospect of unfavorable publicity that may result from being sued. This threat of a suit is sufficient to alarm a businessperson.

Although namedropping and threatening to sue often gets good results, do not expect it to work every time. Perhaps the person that you are up against is really tough, or couldn't care less, or just may not believe you.

Among some common situations that you may be able to handle by yourself are traffic offenses, buyer-seller relationships and drawing up a will. These and others will be covered in the next chapters.

How to Handle
Traffic Offenses

5

When a traffic policeman flags you down and starts to give you a ticket, what do you do? Is there any way to get him to let you off with a warning? Can you maneuver him out of writing the ticket or talk him into voiding it after he's started to write it? What can you do to create a good impression so the police officer may be predisposed to go easy on you?

The first step, when you are flagged down by a police car, is to *get out of your car at once* and go to the police cruiser. This simple act alone makes it more likely that the police officer will let you off with only a warning. The reason is this: The greatest fear a police officer has when he approaches an automobile that has been pulled over is that the driver of the car will shoot him. When you get out of your car, the officer has reason to assume that you're not a dangerous criminal and not his enemy.

Police hear almost every day of an arresting officer being shot to death by a person in an automobile that the officer had flagged down for speeding. It is a constant fear and a very real danger to an officer. The person flagged down may be transporting dope and concerned that the car may be searched; he may believe that he is being stopped for some more serious offense than speeding. Hardened criminals who are wanted by the law and panicky amateurs fearing arrest often don't take the chance that it's just a speeding ticket. They shoot and flee as fast as they can.

THE TIME FOR STRATEGY

Strategy should be used before the officer starts writing the ticket. It is important to talk with the officer before he starts to write the ticket. Many police departments have numbered tickets, and each number must be accounted for. Once written, there is little that can be done to void the ticket—yet even this can be done. Even if the officer has started to write a numbered ticket, he may void it, claiming a mistake. This possibility alone makes it worthwhile to try your strategic moves.

Suppose you are flagged down by a police officer for an offense you feel is unjustified. The officer says that you were going 50 miles an hour in a 35-mile-an-hour zone. You don't believe you were going that fast, but he claims that he "clocked" you on his radar. What should you do?

You must quickly make it clear that an error has been made and that you were not speeding and that you will contest it. If necessary, you can question the calibration of his radar or claim equipment error. (Don't question his skill. You'll merely antagonize him. Without mentioning the possibility of personal error, you can create doubt concerning the equipment.) Police radars are often inaccurate. Unless the equipment is calibrated daily it may not register speed accurately. If the equipment is not operated skillfully by the police officer, the reading may likewise be inaccurate. The police department and the radar operating officer are well aware of this. In fact, because of court challenges, some police departments around the country have suspended radar-clocked speeding arrests.

In a recent case a Dade County (Miami, Florida) judge ruled that radar has not been proved reliable and that radar clockings cannot be used as evidence against speeders. The judge sidetracked nearly a thousand speeding cases after viewing films broadcast by Miami television station WTVJ. The films showed radar units clocking a tree at 86 miles an hour and a house at 28. The judge cited erroneous radar readings caused by interference from such things as billboards, overpasses, CB radios, automobile heaters and air conditioning fans, and police radios. Expert defense witnesses said other errors can be caused by signals from a telephone paging device, two-way radio signals, or simply whistling into the microphone of a citizens' band radio. Further, policemen are often sent out with virtually no training in handling radar units. Interestingly, the prosecutors did not dispute that there might be room for improvement in both equipment and police training. This ruling by the Florida judge is expected to affect rulings in other jurisdictions as well because of the widespread publicity.

Also recently, the Wisconsin Supreme Court reversed a speeding conviction, the High Court ruling that moving radar devices are not so readily accepted in the scientific and engineering community, and that the prosecution must prove the device's accuracy. (*State v. Hanson,* 270 N.E. 2d 212 [1978].)

If a lawyer were representing you in court in a speeding case, he would question the calibration of the radar instrument and the skill of the operator as well. The result might well be an acquittal. You can on the same basis challenge the equipment— and perhaps avoid the ticket. (You *do not* at this time question the officer's skill. You want to stay in his good graces, if possible.) However, if you have to go to court and if you want to handle the case yourself, you will have to do some homework. Your public library may have books on police radars that you will want to look at. If you have a friend in a police department or who is a police prosecutor (preferably from a jurisdiction other than where you have received the ticket) you should try to pick his brains. He will outfit you with all the necessary questions to ask. If your library does not have a book covering speed radars, a good book store will probably have what you want.

BUT YOU DON'T WANT TO GO TO COURT

. . . And neither does the arresting officer. Going to court to contest a traffic citation is the last thing you want to do, of course. It is also the last thing the arresting officer wants to happen. In fact, no person involved in the traffic enforcement division wants you in court contesting the case. You, therefore, have a tremendous leverage working for you.

If the police officer thinks you will dispute the ticket and fight it in court, he may well not issue you the ticket, or he may void it (as a "mistake").

When you contest a traffic citation you throw a monkey wrench into the gears of the machinery of "justice." Traffic courts are designed to handle offenders on a production-line basis. The guilty are fined and disposed of. They are there to pay their fines and take their punishment.

A contested case slows this machinery to a crawl. Evidence must be presented. This means that the traffic officer who clocked your speed must appear to give his evidence. Most police officers do not want to get tied up in a case that involves testifying in court. Their time is involved. Often the case comes up on their day off. A court appearance may interfere with their moonlighting jobs. Likewise, most police chiefs don't want their men tied up in court. The police officer may have to wait a long time before he is called on to testify. It is a waste of personnel time.

It's even worse for them if you have a lawyer representing you. Without a lawyer you'll be much easier to intimidate. But a lawyer can slow the whole process down to a grinding halt. The arresting officer knows that a lawyer can ask all kinds of embarrassing questions, many of which he cannot answer satisfactorily. A lawyer puts the police department on the defensive. He may ask for a postponement, creating an annoying delay. If the offense charge is such that you are entitled to a trial by a jury, the lawyer will ask for a jury. This means an automatic postponement and more wasted time for police personnel—and another trip to court for the arresting officer.

Is it any wonder, then, that a police officer with even the probability of having to go to court will change his mind and give you either an oral or written warning instead? Some police are not even subtle about why they change their mind. My daughter used to have a heavy foot on the accelerator. Once while I was riding with her, she got caught in a speed trap. It was the usual speed trap—no valid reason for the 35-mile-an-hour posted speed limit; a purely money-making project. When I informed the policeman who was preparing to issue a summons that I was contesting the claim of speed, the other police officer blurted, "For God's sake let's not get tied up in court." The officer stopped writing, warned my daughter to watch her speed, and waved her on her way. At no time were either of the police officers aware that I was a lawyer.

Remember this, though: *You have to be convincing about contesting the ticket.* These maneuvers will not work if the officer is not convinced that you mean business.

THERE IS ONE CASE WHERE NOTHING WILL WORK

If you are a long way from home, or if you have out-of-state license plates, the police officer knows that you aren't going to come back to his ticketing preserve just to save a small fine. Policemen know that for most traffic offenses, the economics are against your employing a lawyer. The fine would be less than the lawyer's fee. However, policemen are well aware that some people will spend any amount of money when "it's a matter of principle." They recognize that certain people regularly employ legal counsel, and that counsel will represent them on even minor charges. Some businessmen may have a regularly employed law firm that will furnish counsel without charge. The president of a large corporation may not have to pay the lawyer out of his own pocket. If you convincingly indicate that you have a regularly employed lawyer and that you will have him contest the summons regardless of the cost, the policeman may stop writing the ticket.

Be tactful, but firm. Do not antagonize the officer. But make it clear that an error has been made, that you were not speeding, that you think his radar is defective, that you will contest the traffic citation, and that your lawyer will represent you in court. (It helps if you're driving an expensive, late-model car. If you're driving an old junker, he'll know you're bluffing.)

Even if you're "guilty," you can contest a traffic ticket. Even though you were clearly exceeding the speed limit, do not give up hope. In many states the posted speed limit is not absolute. It is what is called a "prima facie speed limit." This means that though you have exceeded the posted limit, you are only prima facie (not absolutely) guilty of speeding. If you have not endangered anyone, you have not legally violated the intent of the speed limit law. For example, if there is little traffic on a wide road and you are driving safely under the road conditions, you have not violated the intent of the law, even though you've exceeded the posted speed. So, *if your speed has not endangered anyone, and was perfectly safe under the circumstances,* be sure to call it to the officer's attention. He may let you off with a warning. Even in places where the posted speed limit is absolute and not prima facie, many judges will let you off unless you were greatly in excess of the speed limit or are deemed to have endangered others.

IF YOU HAVE TO GO TO COURT

If your maneuvers with the arresting officer have failed and you receive a summons to appear in court, consider carefully. Is your right to drive jeopardized? Could your license be taken away from you if the charges against you are proved? Could you be jailed? Is it important to you to retain the privilege of driving? If so, you would be wise to secure the assistance of a lawyer. But if you have the time and driving isn't important to you and the consequences of losing the case may be minor—go ahead and take your chances in court. Your chances may be better than you think.

To secure the best results possible, you must do some homework. Most public libraries have books containing the local traffic code. You should read the traffic code (laws) that may be applicable. The local courts also have code books. If you have time, make a trip to the court library. By knowing your rights, you'll gain the respect of the judge and the prosecutor. It won't hurt your case if you let both judge and prosecutor learn that you have taken the time to look up the applicable laws. They will respect your rights much more . . . and they may deal with you more leniently. You will have set the stage for your own plea bargaining.

In most jurisdictions minor traffic offenses are tried before a judge only. However, when the offense is serious (such as driving while intoxicated), you may be entitled to be tried by a jury (because you might lose your right to drive or may be sent to jail). A request for a trial by jury throws most traffic courts into a turmoil. Traffic courts seldom try cases using juries, and they do not have jurors readily available. Jurors must be summoned. There will be delays. Often prospective jurors don't show or have good cause to be excused. As a result, it is often difficult for the court to secure a full panel; that is, the number of jurors you are entitled to for a decision in your case. (It varies; the number may be six, nine, or twelve.)

In many traffic courts the judge may have had little or no experience in handling juries; he may not know how to handle a jury case. A jury case entails lots of time and extra work, such as preparing the charges.

For all of these reasons, when you demand a trial by jury (if you are so entitled) you may be able to secure a reduction in the charges against you (even though you are clearly guilty) with a plea of guilty to a lesser offense.

How to Handle
Purchaser-Seller Problems

6

Purchases of products and services—especially purchases that involve substantial amounts of money—often give rise to problems of a legal nature. Some of these you probably can handle on your own. Often, though, you would do well to be represented by a lawyer. The amount of money and grief that he may save you may well be worth many times his fee.

PURCHASES THAT REQUIRE A PURCHASE AGREEMENT

Purchases of products and services that involve a substantial amount of money—for example, purchasing a car or a home, remodeling your home, painting your house, purchasing a business—usually require a purchase agreement. Here are some suggestions on how to handle purchase agreements on your own. (For *very* substantial purchases—such as a business or a home—it would be wise to have the services of a lawyer.)

The salesman who is trying to sell you his product or

services will often make glowing claims for whatever he is selling to induce you to buy. These are often exaggerated and sometimes simply not true. Later, when using the product (or being rendered the service) you discover that it does not conform to the claims made for it.

For example, the used car that you were assured had never been driven over 35 miles an hour by a widow who only used it to go shopping actually belonged to a traveling salesman who drove it hard and put on many more miles than were registered on the mileage meter. You were also assured that the car was so well built that you could drive it another 50,000 miles without its needing motor or body work, aside from a minor tune-up. One thousand miles and two months later you are advised that the engine needs a major overhaul, and there is severe rust damage *under the paint* that will require lots of body work and a new paint job.

You take the car back to the dealer and ask for the return of your money. You will promptly be reminded that the purchase agreement that you signed stated that the written agreement entered into is as stated, and it contains all the terms agreed to and no representations other than those noted therein (none were noted). A further provision states that the purchaser accepts the car in "as-is condition."

What can you do about it? The verbal representations about how well built the car was and that it would not need any major body or engine repair for 50,000 miles, even if proved, generally will not entitle you to any relief. Furthermore, you will not even be allowed to introduce evidence about these claims, since they were not part of the written contract. You cannot introduce oral evidence to change a written contract.

The misrepresentation of the previous ownership and use could be considered fraud in the *inducement*—background material presented to explain reasons for legal action—and if proved could void the contract. Unfortunately, it would be your word against the salesman's word, and, of course, he will deny any such representation. Furthermore, taking the car in "as-is condition" may well prove to be an effective block to relief, even if the judge or jury were to believe you.

If the previous ownership is important to you, you should ask the salesman to state his representation in writing as part of the contract. If the sound condition of the body and motor are likewise important, you should ask for such statements as part of the written purchase agreement. In your acceptance, you should write in that the representations made were relied upon by you. If the representations prove to be untrue, you will then have a legal means of avoiding the agreement, providing they are considered material.

In the example above, it's probable that the used car salesman will not agree to put any of these claims in writing. The example is used merely to illustrate the difference between oral representations and the way they are treated legally. In many transactions you can get the person who wishes to sell you the product or services to make the oral representations—if true—part of the contract.

For example, a painting contractor represents to you that a much more expensive paint he wants to use will not peel or become dirty looking within three years. He may be willing to so state in the contract. If he does and the paint starts to peel and discolor within a year, you should be successful in obtaining relief by a court. The court may award you money to compensate for your damages.

Time allowed for performance of a contract may be of importance to you. In such event you should set out the allotted time for performance in the agreement. For example, you wish to add a new room to your house. You need it within two months, and the contractor represents that he will have it finished within one month. Be sure to have his representations included as part of the contract. Otherwise, you might sit there with a legally binding contract for a room that may not be completed for many, many months—and you may have no legal recourse whatsoever.

What we have already stated applies equally to the purchase of a business. Suppose you are offered the opportunity to purchase a pushcart hot-dog-vending business that is usually located in front of a leading hotel. You believe the business you are purchasing is not important enough to justify consulting a lawyer. The seller represents that he has a city license authorizing operation of the vending business and that it is transferable to you at your request. He represents that the license permits him to occupy the sidewalk in front of the hotel. He also assures you that he clears in excess of $1500 a month.

To avoid disappointment, be sure that the agreement recites these representations. Have it put in writing. Then, of course, before you pay him the purchase price, check the representation out as best you can. If he refuses to put his representations in writing as part of the purchase agreement, then you can forget about the purchase—obviously, his representations are either exaggerated or simply not true.

Many products and services that you are asked to purchase have beautifully illustrated circulars describing the benefits, specifications, and advantages of these products and services and what they will do. Be sure that the purchase agreement refers to these as part of the agreement. If the seller refuses to make a beautiful printed circular part of the agreement by simply referring to it in the agreement and attaching a copy of it to the agreement, you can be assured that the product or service probably will not live up to the representations.

If you sign a purchase agreement that contains notations about the representations and incorporates the illustrated circular, and if what you purchased does not live up to representations made, you are in a strong position to do something legal about it. The first step is to write a letter to the vendor and manufacturer calling the failure to his attention and enclosing a photostatic copy. If you don't get proper adjustment or replacement of the product, you are in a strong position to get it rectified through the courts.

PURCHASES THAT DO NOT LIVE UP TO EXPECTATIONS

Probably the most frequent and troublesome problem most of us encounter is the product that does not live up to expectations. Your new car gives you nothing but trouble, and the dealer doesn't seem to be doing his best; your toaster oven stops working long before the warranty period has run out, but the discount store where you purchased it isn't interested in your problem; your new power lawn mower just won't start, and your dealer shrugs his shoulders. What can you do?

When you purchase a device such as an appliance or an automobile, you receive a document called a *warranty*. Such documents today are usually designated *limited warranty*. This means that only certain problems are covered and usually for a limited period of time.

Read your warranty to see if your problem is covered and to ascertain that it has developed within the warranty period. If you have any doubt and don't understand the language (which may well even confuse a lawyer), *proceed on the theory that your problem is covered.* An elementary rule of law is that where someone draws an agreement that is ambiguous, the ambiguity will be construed against the author. As these warranties are contracts drawn by the manufacturer, the manufacturer is responsible for the confusing language; if there is any question, it will be resolved *against the manufacturer.*

You can get an adjustment or a replacement of the product without having to hire a lawyer if your problem occurs within the warranty provisions or the warranty provisions are ambiguous. You have many practical ways open to you.

Start with your dealer. Reputable dealers will try to make good on any product that was purchased from them. Most warranty provisions require that the appliance must be returned to the manufacturer for service or replacement. A reputable dealer will handle the return of the product for you. However, some dealers, especially discount stores, won't give you this service. They will tell you to return it yourself, that it is not their responsibility.

The store that sold the product to you does have a responsibility to sell you a product without defects. This means, in most jurisdictions, that *if the product isn't satisfactory and proper steps are not taken to satisfy you, you can make a legal claim against the retailer.* If you have to bring suit to enforce your rights, you can sue the retailer, even though the defective product was not manufactured by the retailer. The retailer, of course, has the right to bring into the litigation the manufacturer, who is often located in a distant state. The important thing to you is that your retailer may be just around the corner from you.

So, if the dealer tells you to send the product back to the manufacturer and washes his hands of all responsibility, *you don't have to do it that way.* You can, if you choose, sue him in the locality where you live. And if you desire, you may be able to also sue the manufacturer as part of the same lawsuit.

REPLACEMENT OF A PRODUCT

If the product proves defective shortly after you purchased it and you don't wish to be without the product while it is being repaired by the manufacturer, you may insist on the product being replaced. Most reputable dealers will promptly do so. If you are being shoved around, you may use the magic words "My lawyer" and/or "I will sue."

If you're dealing with a department store, you may wish to write a letter to the attention of the president of the store. You will be surprised how quickly this tactic will get service.

CONSUMER AGENCIES MAY HELP YOU

Another course available to you is to write or call the consumer agency that has jurisdiction. The U.S. government has many different agencies that look after consumers' rights. Some states and large cities have similar agencies. If you live in a large city, look in your telephone book under "U.S. Government," under the state name, and under the city name for a list of consumer agencies located in your city. Many do not have offices in all cities. You may have to go to your public library. The librarian can assist you. Even the smallest libraries have books (usually printed by the U.S. government) that list the various consumer agencies.

When you deal with a government agency by telephone the following procedure will help you get results.

Say: "I wish to speak with someone who can give me advice about (name your problem)."

You will be transferred to another department—usually. After the first transfer of your call you state, "This is Mr. (Mrs. or Miss) Smith. What is your name, please?" If you do this at first, and make sure that you have the name of the person with the correct spelling, you'll get alert attention. Government employees are put on guard when you ask for their names. And it helps you get results, because the person you are talking with has no way of knowing how important you are or what you might do to his agency—so he or she will be very helpful.

It's always helpful to let the dealer know what you are going to do, inasmuch as you are not receiving a proper adjustment on the defective product. Often, just telling the dealer what you plan to do may get results. Inform him that (1) you will get in touch with the appropriate consumer agency regarding the problem; (2) that you will see your lawyer; (3) that you will sue (which we will discuss subsequently).

If you decide to write to a consumer agency, be sure to send a copy of your letter to the dealer and to the manufacturer. You will be surprised how often this will bring you quick service—often even before the government agency has your letter.

Another avenue open to you is to write to the manufacturer and send a copy of the letter to the dealer. A dealer who has many complaints of not servicing his customers may have difficulty continuing to be a dealer. Although it is not ordinarily easy for a manufacturer to discontinue a dealer (because of the legal problems that may be involved), manufacturers can discontinue dealers for cause when the dealer is not properly serving the company's product. This is particularly true in automobile agencies.

YOU MAY HAVE TO SUE

You may, as a last resort, consider filing suit. Every large city has a Small Claims Court. It is a very simple matter to bring suit for the defective product.

Most reputable merchants will do almost anything to avoid suits against them. In addition to the cost of a lawyer and the court costs, the publicity may hurt them.

How to Handle
Your Own Lawsuit

7

You have the right to use the courts without an attorney. You can be your own lawyer. You may sue anyone against whom you think you have a cause of action, within limits. Bringing your own lawsuit is a simple matter in many cases, and the possible problems can be solved without the assistance of a lawyer.

Weigh the matter carefully. Consider the following factors.

You should not resort to a lawsuit if the problem can be solved in any other way. If you do so, you risk the possibility that your lawsuit can backfire on you and bring about a countersuit.

If the amount that you have at stake is substantial, you should get an attorney to handle the lawsuit. His fee in such a case will be well justified by the amount involved.

You should handle only those lawsuits that are not important enough to you to make it worthwhile to hire a lawyer.

BE SURE YOU ARE ENTITLED TO SUE

You are entitled to use the courts without an attorney and sue anyone you feel you have a cause of action against, provided the following conditions are met:

1. Your lawsuit must be *timely.*
2. The court must have *jurisdiction* over the person you are suing.
3. The court must have *power* to handle the matter.
4. The court must be *willing* to accept your lawsuit.

1. Your Lawsuit Must Be Timely

A lawsuit is timely if your rights to sue have not expired due to the passage of time. In legal circles we refer to this time barrier as the *Statute of Limitations.* All causes of action (the rights you have under law) have a period of time within which you must enter your suit or be forever barred.

The reason why we have statutes of limitations is that if we didn't, you (and everyone else) would have to spend the rest of your life worrying about your past mistakes and possible lawsuits. Not only would you have to worry about long-ago mistakes that might become lawsuits any time but also, and even worse, you would be open to an endless number of fraudulent lawsuits that you could not disprove. Because of the long passage of time, witnesses might no longer be available.

For example, suppose you were involved in an automobile accident with a truck. The driver of the truck disregarded the traffic signal that commanded him to stop. Two disinterested witnesses saw the accident, gave you their names and addresses, and said that they were favorable to you. Suppose that ten years later the driver of the truck sues you, alleging that you ran the red light, completely opposite to the facts of the matter. In the meantime, your two witnesses have moved to parts unknown to you or are, perhaps, dead. Now it is his word against yours. It is just as likely that he will be believed as you.

Fortunately, there is a statute of limitations on this kind of action that in many states is two years. (There are exceptions.)

The truck driver would have to sue within two years. If he does sue you within the two-year period, it is less likely that your witnesses may not be available.

Since this is a chapter on bringing your own lawsuit, we will consider the Statute of Limitations from that standpoint.

Suppose you hear from several of your neighbors that your next-door neighbor has said some very nasty—and untrue— things about you, which you believe are slanderous. As a result of these false statements, several neighbors refuse to have anything to do with you. They won't even allow their kids to play with your kids. You are angry about the slanderous statements, because they are not true and they are harming you. You, therefore, consider suing the next-door neighbor for slander. The so-called slanderous statements were made 11 months ago.

If the Statute of Limitations for slander in your state is one year, you will have to file your suit in the appropriate court within 12 months. If you delay until more than 12 months have passed, the Statute of Limitations will have expired. Any suit filed after this expiration will be dismissed. The reason: Your lawsuit was not timely.

The Statute of Limitations varies for different causes of action and for different states; contracts may vary from 6 to 12 years, property damage may be 4 years. *The first thing that you must do is find out what the Statute of Limitations is in your state for the kind of suit that you contemplate bringing*. You can find out by consulting the local clerk of courts, a court library, perhaps even your public library. The important thing is that if you believe you have a cause of action against someone, *you must not procrastinate*—you must enter suit prior to the expiration of the Statute of Limitations.

2. The Court Must Have Jurisdiction over the Person You Are Suing

''Person'' means anyone that you are suing—a corporation, the government, or an individual. All courts have limitations on their jurisdictions. Generally, courts only have jurisdiction over people who live within the geographic area where the court is authorized to transact business. Thus, if you are contemplating using a municipal court in your city, you generally can sue only those people who live within the city. Likewise, if you have a county court whose jurisdiction is limited to that county, you may sue only those who live or are found within the county. However, if the person you want to sue lives in another county, you can always go to that county's court and thus get jurisdiction over the person you are suing.

Courts also may have jurisdiction if certain *events occurred within their geographic area.* For example, when an auto accident occurs within your county, your countywide court may have jurisdiction, even though the motorist you wish to sue does not live in the county. In fact, the court may even have jurisdiction—because of special state laws—over a motorist who resides in another state. Such a law is often referred to as a *Long Arm Statute.* Using Long Arm laws can be tricky—your clerk of courts can answer your questions about invoking such laws.

For information about the various courts, see chapter 26.

3. The Court Must Have Power to Handle the Matter

The court that you wish to use *may have jurisdiction* over the person that you want to sue, but *it may not have the power* to do so. For example, the probate court of your county has jurisdiction over the people who live in the county. However, it only has jurisdiction on probate matters—that is, the handling of estates of deceased people, minors, incompetents, etc., and settlements of related matters. If you want to sue another motorist because you believe he was careless and, as a result, you were injured, you will be in the wrong court if you try to use the probate court. Similarly, you wouldn't bring an accident case to bankruptcy court. They may have jurisdiction over local people, but obviously not over accident cases. The local clerk of courts will assist you in selecting the appropriate court.

4. The Court Must Be Willing To Accept Your Lawsuit

Some courts are limited to a maximum dollar amount. For example, many municipal courts are limited to a maximum of $5000. This means that if you wish to sue your neighbor for slander in the amount of $10,000 in a court with a $5000 limitation, you will be over its jurisdiction. You would then have two choices. One is to revise your suit to $5000, the other is to go to a court of unlimited jurisdiction. The term *court of unlimited jurisdiction* means that the court can handle any kind of cases (with some exceptions, such as probate matters) in any amount and may also have jurisdiction within the entire state. Such courts are called by different names that vary with the state, and they may have various jurisdictional limitations. (See chapter 26.)

Some courts will not handle a lawsuit that is for less than a certain set amount. For example, you cannot go to a United States District Court and sue someone for $500. The United States District Court may have jurisdiction, but it will refuse to accept the filing of your lawsuit. Such a court requires that a far greater amount be sued for. You will have to go to some other court where a $500 suit will be accepted. Generally, the Federal (U.S.) courts can involve you in some very tricky questions as to jurisdiction and another problem referred to as *venue*. Accordingly, it is recommended that you do not use a Federal District Court for cases you handle yourself.

If your locality has what is generally called a *Small Claims Court,* you will want to use it. Such a court is especially set up for people to handle their own lawsuits. In many places it is a division of an unlimited-jurisdiction court system. It may also be a division of a municipal court. Such a Court has a maximum amount set for lawsuits that it may handle. In some places, this amount is under $250, in others $1000, and in some areas even greater.

Usually, such a court has a clerk who will assist you to file and handle your claim. You merely file a simple statement of your claim, and you personally have to appear in court to seek a judgment against the person that you have sued. Most such courts do not allow either you or the person you have sued to have an attorney. The reason for this is that they do not want either party to have an unfair advantage. The filing fee for such court is nominal, probably $1 to $10.

In some parts of the country, *Justice-of-Peace Courts* are still operating. Generally, such courts are tending to disappear, as the reason for their existence is disappearing. Justice-of-

Peace Courts were set up to administer local justice in the days when communities were isolated and travel was difficult and time-consuming. They were originally set up to handle minor disputes, frequently for less than $500.

HOW TO PREPARE YOUR OWN COMPLAINT

Most courts require only that you state a "cause of action" in simple concise language. *Cause of action* means a statement of facts as to why you believe you are entitled to a judgment against the person you have sued. This "person" is referred to as the *defendant*. You are referred to as the *plaintiff* or the *complainant*.

For example, suppose your neighbor has purchased your old lawn mower for $50 but has failed to pay you. Your cause of action can be stated as follows:

> Now comes the complainant and says that on January 4, 1979, he sold defendant, Joe Blow, a lawn mower for the sum of $50, payable within one month. Four months later, defendant has failed to remit the agreed $50. Plaintiff prays for judgment in the sum of $50, together with interest from the 4th day of February, 1979, at the rate of 6%, together with his Court costs.

Another example: Suppose you had purchased a BE toaster for $18.50 from the ABC Discount Store, and three weeks later, it no longer would toast bread. You promptly went to the ABC Discount Store and sought to return the toaster and obtain one that works. ABC refused to take it back and suggested you return it to the manufacturer, as it is guaranteed by them. You asked them to return the toaster to the manufacturer and give you another one. They refused. You can state a cause of action as follows:

> Now comes the plaintiff and for his cause of action against the defendant, ABC, says that on March 11, 1979, he purchased a BE Toaster from the defendant. Said toaster carried a warranty that it would operate satisfactorily for one year. Three weeks after purchased, it would no longer work. Plaintiff sought to have defendant replace the defective toaster. Defendant refused

to honor the warranty or to return the purchase price of $18.50. Wherefore, plaintiff prays for judgment against defendant in the sum of $18.50 along with interest at the rate of 6% plus Court costs.

A third example: The motor on your car was sluggish. You took it to the Fix-It Auto Repair Shop and informed them that it was sluggish and that you would like it taken care of so that it worked properly. That evening you were informed that your car was ready. You were given a bill stating that they replaced the points, adjusted the carburetor, plus a few other items totaling $120 for parts and labor. You paid the bill and drove your car out of the garage and noticed that it was just as sluggish as before. You immediately drove back to the auto repair shop. They informed you that they had done the best they could, that you had an old car and nothing could be done with it short of a complete overhaul. On the way home you stopped at your local gas station and complained about your car. The gas station attendant listened to your motor and told you that it sounded like the spark plugs were not working right. He put in a new set of spark plugs and the motor purred beautifully. The filling station attendant called to your attention that the carburetor showed no sign of having recently been worked on and your points had not been changed. You returned to Fix-It and they refused to refund your $120.

Your cause of action could be stated as follows:

Now comes the plaintiff and says that on January 12, 1979, he took his 1972 Ford automobile into defendant's auto repair shop requesting that the sluggish motor be taken care of. After listening to the motor, defendant's service manager assured him that a light tune-up was all that it needed and that he would take care of it. That afternoon plaintiff was informed that the motor had been tuned and that the motor was now operating properly. Plaintiff was billed $120 for services and parts for the tune-up, which included new points and adjustment of the carburetor, which plaintiff paid in cash. On driving the automobile out of the garage, plaintiff discovered that the motor was still sluggish and promptly returned to the garage calling this to the attention of the service manager. The service manager refused to do anything stating that it was an old car and that nothing more could be done for it except a complete overhaul.

Plaintiff further says that on the way home he stopped to fill his tank with gasoline and was informed by the filling station attendant that it sounded like it needed new spark plugs. Upon changing the spark plugs the motor hummed beautifully. Also the attendant called to plaintiff's attention that the carburetor had not recently been serviced and the points had not been changed.

Plaintiff promptly returned to defendant's garage and called these to the attention of the service manager and requested the return of his $120. Defendant refused.

Plaintiff says that defendant's conduct was fraudulent; that it made representations of having made repairs when in fact none had been made.

WHEREFORE, Plaintiff prays for judgment against defendant in the sum of $120 which he paid for the nonexistent repairs together with $5,000 for punitive damages with interest at the rate of 6% and court costs.*

Generally, you would be entitled only to damages that would compensate you for your loss; in this case $120. However, since the defendant's conduct was malicious and fraudulent, you may be entitled to *punitive damages*. The rationale for punitive damages is to punish someone for malicious, fraudulent, or outrageous conduct. In some states you would not be entitled to punitive damages. Other states will award them. In many states it is not clear whether the courts will or will not award them in situations such as the one described above.

The reason for this uncertainty is that in many states punitive damages are a new type of recovery. If there is any question as to what the law is in your state, you may find it worthwhile to sue for punitive damages anyway. A request for punitive damages does frighten many people, especially those whose conduct is such that the court might grant punitive damages. In such situations, you may find that the defendant will quickly agree to refund your money along with your court costs.

---

*In law libraries and in some public libraries legal form books may be available that have more comprehensive examples that you can follow, if you wish.

THE FORMAT OF YOUR COMPLAINT

Use plain typewriter paper; letter size is generally acceptable. Lawyers use legal size, 8½ by 14 inches. Some courts may be fussy and you may have to use legal size. It is advisable that you check with the clerk of courts of the court that you plan to employ. In addition, ask the clerk if you can see a petition so that you can visualize the format. You might ask him for a copy to use as a guide. Your petition should be typewritten. You will need the original for the court and a copy for each person that you sue, plus a copy for yourself.

Near the top type in the name of the court that you are using. Then skip several spaces. On the left side type in your name and your full address. Skip a few more lines and type in "v.," skip a few more lines and type in the name of the person (or corporation or company) that you are suing. To the right of your and the defendant's names and addresses, identify the relief that you are asking for. Generally, it will be entitled "Complaint (or "Petition") for money only."

An example:

```
                  IN THE COURT OF COMMON PLEAS

                  JACKSONVILLE COUNTY, OHIO

      JOHN DOE              )      CASE NO.
      4435 Main Street      )
      Cleveland, Ohio 44565 )      JUDGE
                            )
            v.              )
                            )
      MARY SMITH            )      COMPLAINT FOR MONEY ONLY
      4325 Pearl Street     )
      Akron, Ohio 44543     )
                            )
            Defendant       )
                            )
```

If the defendant is a corporation, you should so state in the first paragraph, and if you know what state it is incorporated in, also add that information.

If you are suing an out-of-state defendant as a result of an automobile accident, you will have to ask the clerk of courts how to do this. In some states you may have to sue through the secretary of state of your state. Generally, the court operating in the area where the accident occurred has jurisdiction and permits you to legally serve the other motorist, even though he does not reside in your own state.

Likewise, in many states, if *one* of the defendants resides in your area, *you may be entitled to sue and obtain service on a nonresident* of your state. This right may be important if you wish to sue the manufacturer of a defective product whose factory is located in a state other than the one where you live and purchased the product. Thus, if you purchase a defective toaster at your local discount store, most states will permit you to sue the merchant who sold you the defective product, in this case the discount store. Since the discount store is in the locality served by your court, that court will have jurisdiction. You may then also be entitled to sue the manufacturer of the toaster. This may bring you a quicker adjustment or replacement. However, because of the service outside your locality, the court deposit and court costs may be much higher. As it may not be necessary to join the manufacturer (make the manufacturer a defendant also in the suit), it may be wiser for you to simply enter your suit against the discount store.

The discount store will undoubtedly tender the lawsuit to the manufacturer. In most states the retailer selling you the product impliedly warrants that it is not defective and is fit for the purposes for which it was sold, even though he did not manufacture it. (This may not be true in all jurisdictions or for all products. Again, you may have to check with the clerk of courts.) If you are successful against the retailer, he, in turn, would be entitled to collect against the manufacturer. This is often referred to as secondary and primary liability. In some states a retailer may be able to join the manufacturer in your suit.

CLERK OF COURTS

Throughout this section on bringing your own lawsuit you have been advised to consult the clerk of courts *of the court that you plan to use.* The clerk of courts is a public servant, and you are entitled to his assistance, provided you don't make a nuisance of yourself and unduly take up his time or that of his staff. Most clerks of courts will gladly cooperate with you. Some may try to brush you off; if so, be insistent and remind them that you have a right to file a lawsuit and that under the law they are public servants and as such are duty bound to give you reasonable assistance.

SUING CHILDREN

Children cannot be sued directly. The reason for this is that if children are sued, they may not comprehend or know what to do about the suit, even if it lacks merit. Accordingly, if the person is a *minor* (that is, a person who is under the legal age — in some places, under twenty-one; in others, under eighteen), he or she must be sued through a parent or a guardian. This means that you will sue the child and join a parent or a guardian. When you sue a child, you have to state that he or she is a minor and state his or her age (if you know).

FILING FEES

To file a lawsuit with a court, you have to pay a *filing fee*. Filing fees vary from court to court. They may vary from $1 to more than $100. Most likely, the filing fee will range from $10 to $25. Some courts will waive the filing fee if you take a poverty oath.

If you dismiss your suit and the court costs are less than your deposit, the court will usually mail you the difference. If the court costs exceed your deposit, you will be billed. If you settle, it is customary for the defendant to pay the court costs. Upon such payment, the court will refund your entire deposit. If the defendant agrees to pay you, you will usually be asked to sign papers wherein you agree to dismiss the action and release the defendant against your cause of action. Be sure before you sign that the release states that the defendant pays the court costs.

If your case is tried and you win, the court will assess the defendant with the court costs. When the defendant pays the judgment, he will also have to pay the court costs. The court will then mail you your deposit.

If you lose your lawsuit, you will be assessed all court costs. Generally, court deposits will not cover all possible court costs, but are designed to cover costs of serving the defendant and of the various preliminary processes to the point at which the average case is settled. If it is necessary to try the case, the court costs incurred will be considerably in excess of the deposit. You will usually be billed for the amount that the court costs exceed your deposit. If you don't pay, many courts will take steps to collect from you. As court costs often can become quite sizable, it behooves you to take care that you sue only on meritorious matters. Otherwise you will spend a lot of time and effort and have to pay a lot of court costs as well.

THE DEFENDANT

The person that you sue is referred to as the *defendant*. He becomes a defendant after he is served with the summons and a copy of the complaint. Service can be made by a sheriff, bailiff, or other process server, who serves the defendant personally. More usually, it is delivered by registered or certified mail. Many courts use regular mail. Service includes a copy of your complaint.

The summons usually states that unless the defendant answers the complaint against him within the time provided in the summons (frequently three weeks), the complaint will be taken as true. The summons then states that if the complaint is not answered, the court will find that the complaint is true and render judgment in the amount asked for. If the defendant does not respond with an answer, some courts will automatically enter judgment for the amount requested. This is referred to as *a default judgment*.

Other courts will only set up default hearing upon your specific request. Such courts often will send a postcard notifying the defendant that a default hearing will be held on the date assigned. If the defendant appears, he will be heard by the judge. Such courts will require some proof from you that your claim is meritorious, even if the defendant does not appear.

If the defendant contests your complaint, he will most likely secure an attorney to defend. (If you are suing in Small Claims Court, it usually has a rule prohibiting the defendant from having an attorney.) If you are suing a manufacturer he will probably set up affirmative defenses, such as misuse of the product.

CROSS PETITION

Before you sue you must consider the possibility or probability that the defendant may sue you in a *cross petition* (or *counterclaim*) against you. The cross petition can arise from the same transaction or incident that has given rise to your lawsuit. It can also be for something totally unrelated to the event that you complained about. Suppose that you sue your neighbor for the $50 that he failed to pay for the lawn mower that he purchased from you, as cited in a previous example. A counterclaim against you might be made for slander because of slanderous remarks you allegedly made at a neighborhood party. (Some courts on your request, referred to as *a motion,* will dismiss such counterclaim, as it does not arise out of the same incident as your lawsuit.)

A more typical example: you have an intersection accident involving your car and another vehicle. Each of you has claimed that the traffic light was displaying green. Let's assume (as is frequently the situation) there are no disinterested witnesses. It's your word against his. Your car was damaged to the tune of $250 and his for a similar amount; in addition, he has complained of injuries at the scene of the accident. Before you sue him for $250, you must weigh the possibility that he will cross petition against you for his property damage and perhaps even for his personal injury. The amount he sues for may be considerably more than your damages. If he cross petitions, then it may become necessary for you (especially if it's for a sizable sum) to hire a lawyer to defend. Of course, if you have liability insurance on your automobile, you can then turn over the cross petition to your insurance carrier, who will then hire a lawyer at its expense.

If you have no insurance carrier and the defendant cross

petitions, you will then have to prepare an answer to the cross petition denying its allegations. If you have a contested lawsuit, you must do your legal homework. In an accident case you will find it advisable to investigate to find out if any witnesses saw the accident. You will then have to talk to them to find out if they are favorable to you. If they are, you will have to make arrangements for their appearance in court. You can often secure a voluntary appearance or you can use a *subpoena*, a court process that commands the witness to show up in court on the appointed date and time. The clerk of courts will advise you on how to arrange to have a witness subpoenaed. Your court will probably have a bailiff or sheriff serve the subpoena. Usually you have to pay a witness fee and mileage for the witness's transportation in advance. The filing fee for a subpoena may vary from $2 to $25 or more. You also may find it advisable to take pictures of the scene of the accident to show the court how the accident happened.

Before you file a lawsuit, it is advisable to notify the potential defendant that if he does not treat you fairly, you will enter suit against him. Many people get quite concerned about the prospect of being sued and may voluntarily decide to treat you fairly.

COLLECTING YOUR JUDGMENT

If you obtain a judgment against someone, the next problem is collecting it. If the judgment is against an insurance company or other responsible company or individual, it will most likely be paid voluntarily. If the judgment is against a person who will not pay you voluntarily, then you have additional work to do.

The law provides legal avenues you can use to enforce your judgment. In some jurisdictions you have available what is often referred to as an *Aide in Execution*. This usually requires the issuance of a summons from the court for the debtor to appear to answer your questions under oath concerning his assets and employment.

If your debtor is employed and you know the location of the employer, you can then use a proceeding frequently referred to as *garnishment*. The clerk of court can direct you how to file certain papers that will command the debtor's employer to remit a certain percentage of his salary toward payment of the debt. Garnishment laws of the various states differ extensively. Some states permit you to garnish only a certain percentage of the debtor's wages. Other states will not permit garnishment unless the debtor's wages are in excess of a certain amount. The court in which you have obtained a judgment will normally have garnishment forms available that you can use as a guide.

After you have determined what assets the debtor has and whether or not he is employed, you may then wish to *execute on the judgment*. To execute upon a judgment, you direct the sheriff or other local constable in the jurisdiction where the judgment has been obtained to seize the available property of the debtor and to sell the property to satisfy the judgment amount. If the value of the debtor's property is in excess of the judgment amount, only so much of the debtor's property as is required to satisfy the judgment will be sold. The forms for instituting an execution on a judgment are generally also available from the clerk of courts.

When you seek to collect the judgment you may find that the debtor has moved. Sometimes a forwarding address is left and other times not. It is more likely that he will not tell his neighbors where he has moved but will notify the post office. Accordingly, to locate him you will find it worthwhile to mail him a demand letter by certified mail, requesting a receipt showing where the letter was delivered.

If this does not help you locate the debtor, you may find it helpful to phone several of the neighbors who live next door or across the street from his old address. To get the phone numbers of neighbors you can try the city directory, which is usually obtainable in most public libraries. Ask the librarian. The public directory will give you the name but may not give the phone number. You can then refer to the telephone directory. Another directory, if available, is ideal. This is referred to as the *crisscross*. There all city residents are listed by street and number.

How to Handle
Drawing Your Own Will

8

To be valid, your will must comply with all legal formalities required by your state. If you fail in *any* respect, your will may not be considered valid. Your heirs and the probate court may then ignore your wishes and proceed as if you had not left a will. If your will is ignored by the probate court, your property will pass as provided for by your state laws. This may result in your property passing in a way that is contrary to your wishes. It is, therefore, advisable to secure the help of a lawyer to make sure your property will be disposed of the way you wish it to be.

If the property that you leave has sufficient value, state inheritance taxes may have to be paid. Worse yet, federal estate taxes may be assessed. Failure to have a lawyer plan your estate and prepare your will may result in needlessly large taxes.

INHERITANCE TAXES

State laws vary greatly on inheritance taxes. So do exemptions, depending on your marital state, the number of children that you have, etc. It is not possible to give even a rough estimate that will enable you to decide whether your estate is large enough to require payment of inheritance taxes or guess at how much. Generally speaking, if you have an estate equal in value to the average house, you may well have an inheritance tax levied against your estate.

Federal estate tax is also complicated. The size of your estate and any gifts you have given in excess of $3,000 during your lifetime are involved. If you leave any property to your spouse, it makes a difference in the amount of tax. Generally, to be subject to federal estate tax your estate must be a lot larger than the size required to be subject to state inheritance tax, which are comparatively low compared with federal estate taxes.

IF YOU STILL WANT TO MAKE YOUR OWN WILL . . .

If you have considered the drawbacks in making your own will and still wish to do it on your own, here are some suggestions. You must declare your will as being your last will and testament, that you are of sound mind, and that you revoke any wills made previously. You will have to state to whom you are leaving your property. In the event you are leaving your estate to your spouse, you may wish to provide for the possibility that when you die, your spouse may not be living, and you may wish to add the following: "If my _____ shall not survive me, then I bequeath all my property to my children in equal shares. If any of my said children predecease me, the share of such deceased child [or children] shall be divided equally by my surviving child [or children]. My living child or children as of this date are _____." You must also name the person you want to be executor of your estate. (The executor is the person who will have the task of seeing to it that your wishes are carried out.) A common disaster clause (Item IV of the sample will) eliminates problems that could occur in a joint disaster such as an automobile accident and could prevent double taxation and double probate.

```
LAST WILL AND TESTAMENT OF _____

I _____ of _____

being of sound mind make and declare this my last will and testament, hereby

revoking any and all wills that I may have made heretofore.


                              ITEM I

                        PAYMENT OF DEBTS

I direct that all my just debts be paid out of my estate.


                              ITEM II

                       SPECIFIC BEQUESTS

I make the following specific requests; My _____ to my _____. If any of

the beneficiaries named in this item shall not survive me, the bequest to such

beneficiaries shall lapse and shall become a part of my residuary estate hereinafter

disposed of.


                             ITEM III

                        GENERAL BEQUEST

All the rest of the property which I own at the time of my death of whatsoever nature

and wheresoever situated I bequeath to my _____.

If my _____ shall not survive me than I bequeath all my property to my

children in equal shares. If any of my said children predecease me, the share of

such deceased child or children shall be divided equally by my surviving child or

children. My living child or children as of this date are _____.


                             ITEM IV

                     COMMON DISASTER CLAUSE

In the event that any beneficiary hereunder shall die at the same time as I or in a

common disaster with me, or under such circumstances that it is impossible or

difficult to determine who died first, such beneficiary shall be deemed not to have

survived me.
```

If you have children who are minors, you will need to name a guardian for them, as in Item V of the sample will. It is a good idea to check with the person (or persons) you have named as guardian to find out if he or she will agree to accept if confronted with the necessity of acting in the capacity of guardian.

You will need at least two, and perhaps three, witnesses

MINOR CHILDREN

In the event that my _____ (spouse) should predecease me, I request the appointment of _____ as guardian of the person and the estate of each child of mine who may at the time be a minor. If for any reason the above mentioned person is unable to qualify as guardian or after qualifying, shall cease to act in such capacity, I then appoint _____ as the guardian of the person and the estate of each child of mine who may at the time be a minor.

ITEM VI

EXECUTOR (OR EXECUTRIX)

I nominate and appoint _____ as my (executor or executrix) of this my last will and testament hereby granting to (him or her) full power and authority to sell and convey all or any part of my estate, real, personal or mixed, upon such terms as my executor or executrix may deem proper.

In the event that _____ shall for any reason fail to qualify or having qualified, fails to complete the administration of my estate, I nominate and appoint _____ in his or her place giving to _____ all rights and powers set forth in this item.

In witness whereof I have signed published and declared this instrument to be my last will and testament. _____

(Signature)

executed this _____ date at _____.

The foregoing will was signed in our presence, and in the presence of each other, we have hereunder subscribed our names as witnesses this _____ date of.

WITNESSES

_____ RESIDING AT _____

_____ RESIDING AT _____

_____ RESIDING AT _____

(since some jurisdictions require three), none of whom are named in the will to receive money or property. In their presence you will declare this to be your last will and testament and state that you are in sound mind and know what you are doing. They must watch you sign and you must watch them sign. You have no obligation to disclose the contents of your will.

PROBATING A SMALL ESTATE

When someone dies leaving property, the legal machinery for transferring such property to the heirs is handled by a court, usually referred to as the Probate Court, using rules referred to as the Probate Code or Law.

The probate laws of many states provide for exempting very small estates from the necessity of probate. The size of exemption varies from jurisdiction to jurisdiction. So the first thing that you want to do is check to see whether the estate that you wish to probate is exempt and, if so, what is required to effect the exemption and transfer the decedent's property to his heirs at law or his heirs by will.

If the estate is in excess of the exemption, it is wise to obtain the services of a lawyer. A lawyer not only can save you a great deal of grief and lots of work but, even more important, his knowledge of the state and inheritance taxes and of the various exemptions and how you go about obtaining them might save you considerably in excess of his fee. However, if you insist on probating the estate yourself, then your first step is to go to the Probate Court and ask the clerk for the various forms that he requires you to fill out.

Generally, you will start with having to file a copy of the will or a statement to the effect that the decedent left no will, and state your position as an heir or other interested party. If the decedent did not leave a will, then, of course, you must obtain a copy of your state code concerning distribution of property where a decedent has no will. Generally, this can be obtained at your Probate Court.

The court will have various schedules that it wishes to be filled out and filed. You will be required to list all of the decedent's property, along with estimated value. Most Probate Courts will, in addition, require an appraisal by a court-appointed appraiser, who will appraise at your expense.

Generally, the various schedules that you will be required to file must be approved by the Probate Judge. As a practical matter, a busy Probate Court has referees who either approve or disapprove in the judge's name. In less busy courts the referee will bring it to the point where it is ready for the judge's approval. The judge will then check it or just simply sign it.

How to Handle
Your Own Divorce

9

Marriage is a three-way contract. It is a contract between *you, your spouse,* and *the state* in which you live. For many it may be a four-way contract, being also a kind of contract with *your religion.*

Usually contracts can be terminated simply—by mutually agreeing to do so. In most states, marriage cannot be terminated in the same way as other contracts because the state is also involved. Generally the state is interested in three things.

1. That the marriage can be terminated only for certain reasons, which are referred to as *grounds for divorce.*
2. That the welfare of the wife be considered and provided for. Some states are beginning to consider also the welfare of the husband. When existing divorce laws were written the wife was a housewife. She had no outside employment and rarely had her own outside income. For this reason, the state wanted to be sure that she was properly provided for—hence, alimony. With the increase of working women who sometimes earn more than their

husbands, the courts are becoming increasingly concerned with the welfare of the husband when the marriage is dissolved.

3. The state has always been interested in the welfare of the children: Who is to get custody, visitation rights of the other parent, and most important, of course, provision for adequate support.

Between you and your spouse an agreement as to division of property, alimony, custody of children, visitation, and support of the children can often be arrived at. When this is reduced to writing, it is referred to as a *separation agreement.* Generally, the courts will not disturb a fair separation agreement. However, when it comes to the custody of and support for the children, the divorce court (which is referred to in some areas as a Family Court and in others as a Domestic Relations Court) will carefully review the arrangements made and may modify them, depending on what the court determines as being fair.

As previously noted, the state generally will not agree to termination of the marriage unless there is a recognized ground for the divorce. In recent years many states have become increasingly liberal, recognizing that if two people cannot live together as husband and wife, this should be sufficient reason for consenting to the marriage being terminated. Such states are often referred to as *no-fault divorce* states.

Where the laws of your state permit "no-fault divorces," you can often handle the divorce without the aid of a lawyer. However, if you have children, and if you have property to any extent, you would be wiser to secure the services of a lawyer. If alimony is involved, it is even more important that both husband and wife be represented by counsel.

If your state is not a so-called no-fault-divorce-law state and requires definite grounds for divorce and proof that these exist, you have little choice other than to get yourself a lawyer. You can find out where you stand by asking the clerk of courts involved.

If your state has no-fault divorce laws, go to your domestic relations court, or to the domestic relations division, or, as it may be referred to, the Family Law Court for information on how to go about handling your divorce.

How to Handle Job Problems

10

A legal problem may develop at your place of employment. You could be fired and believe that you were unfairly treated. You may have been paid less than the prevailing wage and feel that you are entitled to the difference. You may believe that you have not been promoted because of some form of discrimination—because of your sex, ethnic background, color, religion, or age. These are legal problems that can usually be handled without hiring a lawyer.

MAKE A COMPLAINT

Your state has bureaus or commissions that have been set up to oversee and handle work-related problems. If you have a complaint concerning discriminatory employment—including hiring, upgrading salaries, fringe benefits, promotion, and training—on the basis of sex as well as of race, color, religion or national origin, and if your employer has in excess of 15 employees, you can complain to the nearest regional office of the U.S. Equal Employment Opportunity Commission.

In addition, most states have Human Rights or Fair Employment Practices Commissions. If so, you may wish to register your complaint with the state. Many job-related problems, other than discrimination, are within the jurisdiction of other state and federal bureaus. The Veterans Administration, the Social Security Administration, your State Unemployment Bureau, to mention a few, may have some authority in the matter involved. In addition, if you live in a sizable city, there may be various municipal boards whose duty is to assist you.

START WITH THE TELEPHONE BOOK

The place to start is your phone book. Look under "United States Government." You will find there a list of all the federal governmental agencies with local offices. Frequently the title is descriptive enough for you to determine whether your problem is in their jurisdiction. A call to such a bureau will give you the answer; if that office does not have jurisdiction, the person answering the phone may be able to tell you who does, and give you the number of the office or agency to call.

You will also find state offices that may be helpful in the telephone book. Look under the name of your state. You will find names of various bureaus. Call a likely bureau, and keep calling until you locate the office that can handle your problem.

If you can't find the number in your phone book, try the public library. It will undoubtedly have directories of federal and state government bureaus and boards, as well as your local governmental units. Ask the Librarian for assistance. Usually the directories will have the name and address and the phone number as well. A few phone calls and you should be able to locate the board or bureau that has jurisdiction over your special problem.

If you are discharged for cause from your job, you may not be entitled to unemployment compensation. A branch of the unemployment compensation office located near you can usually answer your questions. But its decision may not be final. If it gives you a decision that you believe is contrary to the way you understand the law as written, there may be a basis provided for you to appeal. The office will tell you how to go about effecting your own appeal.

Be persistent and you may get what you want.

How to Handle Bringing
Your Own Eviction Actions

11

You are owner of some rental property. You have (1) tenants who have become delinquent in their rent, (2) tenants who are undesirable and you want them out, or (3) a need for the premises, either for your own use or for someone else's. How do you go about evicting the tenants?

Although eviction actions are simple, they can become complicated if you have local rent control and/or restricting eviction-action rules. If your area is rent-controlled, the tenant whom you wish to evict may give you trouble. He may claim that you wish to evict him because he is not receptive to an increase in rental that is in excess of the rent-control formula. If rent control is involved, you may find it worthwhile to consult a lawyer. As an alternative, a local clerk of courts may be able to assist you.

Local and state laws on eviction vary so much that you must check to be sure what the local laws are. You must comply with the local legal requirements, otherwise you may not only fail to secure eviction of the tenant but, worse yet, you may subject yourself to a cross petition and various other tenant actions and penalties. The information furnished here will generally apply to many localities, but it may not apply to your particular area. It will give you a rough guide, but it is best to be sure of your local laws before taking action.

Generally, when you wish to evict someone, you must furnish a written notice requesting that the tenant vacate the premises. Some areas permit a three-day notice, other areas may require a week or even more time. In your notice, you must state the reason for eviction. In some areas you merely send a letter regular mail; in others, you must send it by registered mail. In many places, all you have to do is serve a copy of the notice on the tenant or leave a copy under the door of the premises.

If the tenant fails to vacate, then you must file your eviction action in court. At this point, you must consult your local clerk of courts to find what is required and to obtain a sample complaint from him. As a rule, such a complaint is very simple. It recites ownership, the reason for eviction, notice, and failure to vacate the premises. If the tenant owes you for back rental, you will wish to state how much rent he owes you.

Eviction matters usually come up for early hearing, in many courts, in one week. Other courts, of course, may take longer. In eviction actions, the tenant usually does not have to file an answer. If he wishes to contest the eviction, he will show up on the date and at the time specified in the notice. The court will then have a brief hearing.

If the court grants the eviction, and frequently eviction action itself is uncontested, they will give the tenant adequate time to vacate the premises. If the tenant is not present, the court may send him a notice that he is ordered to vacate the premises by such and such a date. If he is present, the tenant will usually plead for adequate time to find another place and to move. The judge may grant him considerable time.

The tenant will, of course, owe you rent for the period of time that he occupies the premises and should pay it. Unfortunately, most tenants, once they're under notice of eviction, rarely bother to pay the rent. This means that when your eviction has been completed and you are owed rent, you then have a collection problem. (Refer to chapter 7 for ways of enforcing your collection and how to handle such problems.)

In many areas, if tenants do not get out on or by the date that they have been ordered to vacate, the court will *not* ask (as was the case years ago) the sheriff to move the tenants' belongings out of your suite or house onto the sidewalk. It rather will require that you make arrangements for a mover and have the tenants' furniture placed in the moving van. This, of course, may mean further delay.

How to Handle Claims Against The Government

12

When you have a claim against a government unit, whether federal, state, or local, the presentation is quite different from a claim against an individual or corporation. In addition, you have the legal right to make claims against individuals and corporations but you may not have the legal right to make claims against all government units. The reason is that our laws developed from ancient English common law, and in ancient England you could not sue the king without his permission. Since the king did not like to be sued, he frequently withheld his permission. When we broke away from England, our government units kept the rule; however, not having a king to grant permission, they simply prohibited suits against the government.

Thus if a government employee on government business carelessly caused a person to be injured, that person's suit against the government would be dismissed on the grounds that you cannot sue the sovereign. Unfortunately, being injured by an employee of the government was just as painful and disabling as being injured by an ordinary citizen. As a result, the courts slowly chipped away at this prohibition. The first distinction was that you could sue a government unit when it was engaged in a proprietary function. Thus if your municipality had a municipal light plant, which is considered a proprietary function, you could sue the municipality for the negligence of an employee.

In some states the courts in recent years have eliminated the immunity of additional government units, using various reasons. In addition, in many states the legislature changed the rules regarding suits against some government units. Some states passed laws providing for special claims boards, sometimes referred to as the Sundrys Claims Board or as a Moral Claim Board.

Many laws by the various states do not permit you to sue the government unit, but you can present your claim. If you are turned down, you usually have no appeal, in contrast to your right to appeal a court's decision. In addition, you depend not on rules of law but on the generosity or lack of generosity of the particular board.

If you are seriously injured as a result of the carelessness of a government employee on government business, you would be well advised to secure the services of a lawyer. He will know whether you can make a claim, against whom you can make the claim, and how you go about making the claim.

If you want to do it on your own, you may well wish to contact the government unit whose employee caused your injury. You may write the government unit a letter stating that you have been injured as a result of the carelessness of its employee. You will, of course, include the date, the name of the employee, and where the accident occurred. Usually you will hear from a central claim or legal department that handles claims for all government units of that particular municipality or state. This department will usually send you a form that may be labeled "statement of claim." The form asks how the accident occurred, the nature of the injury, amounts of medical bills, etc. Upon receiving your filled-in form, the department may process it to the point of payment. Usually, some kind of hearing will be scheduled and you will be asked to appear and state your case.

Unfortunately many government units do not function very efficiently. You may receive no response. All government units that permit claims usually have statutes of limitations within which you must make the claim. This means that if you do not hear within a reasonable period of time, it is important that you follow up to find out what happened to your claim.

Frequently, if your claim is against a municipality, the municipality law department can usually brief you on how to go about presenting your claim. If a state is involved, a telephone call or visit to the appropriate department or even the state attorney general's office may be in order.

Some localities will reimburse you for property damage. For example, if you are driving your automobile on a city street and hit a very big chuckhole and break your wheel, you may find that your municipality will reimburse you for the damage. However, claims against the government are principally designed to take care of personal injury.

Claims against the federal government are handled under what is referred to as the Federal Tort Claims Act. The Federal Tort Claims Act is quite involved; if you are injured as a result of the carelessness of an employee of the federal government, your local federal district attorney can tell you how to present your claim. Generally, you will write to the bureau or subdivision responsible. For example, if you are injured as a result of the carelessness of a post office employee while driving a post office truck you will make your claim in writing to the post office. If you don't hear from the post office in reasonable time or as a result of a follow-up letter, you may have to petition under the Federal Tort Claims Act. The petition is a suit against the government, but you are not entitled to a jury.

How to Handle
Personal Injury

13

Personal injury is so common, you may wish to know what to do if you are injured under circumstances in which you believe someone else is at fault.

Suppose you are injured. You believe that someone else is at fault, and you believe that they or their insurance carrier should compensate you. Your injury may have been caused by an automobile accident or may have happened on someone else's premises. It may have been caused by a machine, a product, or someone's malpractice. Personal injury may occur in any number of ways. The person or company you believe responsible may be covered by insurance or may have no insurance coverage.

The obvious question is, "Do I need a lawyer?" or "Can I handle my claim myself, without the services of a lawyer?"

When a person (or a company) is insured, he or she is required under the insurance policy to promptly notify the insurance company of the accident. The insurance company then will investigate the accident to determine who, if anyone, was at fault. Unfortunately, many people, even if they know they are at fault, hate to admit it and will often blame other people or other things. They may not even bother to report the accident.

The first thing an insurance company does is find out what happened from the insured person's viewpoint. It secures the assured's version of what happened. The insurance company also asks for the names of witnesses and obtains a copy of the police report, if one was made. The insurance company will interview the witnesses, if it is deemed necessary. If the insurance company is satisfied that its insured was not at fault, it may not bother to contact you. If there is any doubt, it will contact you to obtain your version of what happened and the names of any witnesses that you may have obtained.

In such event, you will either be contacted in person or by telephone by a representative of the insurance company. Most likely, the investigator will record the conversation with you. The investigator will be interested not only in how the accident happened but also whether you were injured and, if so, to what extent.

You will find it in your best interests to answer the questions as honestly as you can. If you don't understand any question, be sure that you so state. If you cannot answer any question, be sure to tell the interviewer. If you're called upon to guess, make it clear that you are guessing. Some people, instead of answering the questions truthfully, answer them in a way that they hope will shift the blame to the other party. This is a mistake. Insurance company investigators and their supervisors can often detect whether or not you are telling the truth. By not telling the truth, you may put yourself as well as the insurance company to lots of trouble and expense without material benefit to yourself.

If you have a lawyer, you should so advise the investigator at once, and he will not question you any further. Your lawyer will represent you. The insurance companies and the American Bar Association appointed a committee that has issued a statement of principles on respective rights and duties of lawyers, insurance companies, and adjusters relating to the business of adjusting insurance claims. This agreement states:

The committee believes that anyone that has, or thinks he has, a claim against a company is entitled at all times to courteous, fair, and just treatment from the representative of the company. A claimant [this is you if you are making a claim] is entitled to an investigation of his claim and a reasonable prompt statement of the company's position with reference to it. . . . The committee recognizes that while the companies have a definite obligation to pay all just claims and to avoid unnecessary litigation, they have an equally definite obligation to protect the insurance-buying public from increased costs due to the fraudulent or nonmeritorious claims.

Under this agreement you or any witness making a signed statement will be given a copy of such statement upon request.

In this agreement, companies or their representatives have agreed that they will not advise a claimant against seeking legal advice or against retention of counsel to protect his interest. They further agree that companies will respect the disabilities of minors and incompetents and agree that no settlement of a cause of action of an infant or of an incompetent shall be presented to the court for approval except under provision for investigation of the propriety of the settlement, either by the court or by counsel independent of the defendant.

You will note that the preceding paragraph states that the agreement provides that a company or its representative should not advise you to refrain from seeking legal advice or advise you against the retention of counsel to protect your interest. This does not mean that you should secure counsel just because you have been injured. However, should a representative of an insurance company advise you not to get a lawyer's advice to protect your interest, you should seriously consider securing counsel. The reason is that when the representative breaches his agreement, you would do well to evaluate his honesty in dealing with you.

You must bear in mind that insurance companies are in the business of adjusting meritorious claims against their assureds. Good insurance companies have long ago discovered that it is bad business to be unreasonable in the settlement of claims. If the amount of the settlement is unconscionably low, the company knows that such a low settlement may be set aside by a court. If the insurance company is unreasonable in dealing with you, it knows that this will tend to drive you to obtain counsel.

For this reason, most insurance companies will try to be as fair to you as they can.

This does not necessarily mean that they will pay you as much money as they would pay if you were represented by counsel. They know that if you are represented by counsel, that counsel must be paid. The company thinks in terms of what you would receive after deducting lawyer's fees and expenses that may be involved in presenting your claim. This is frequently the basis of a direct offer to settle.

It is in your best interests to give the insurance company a reasonable opportunity to make a fair settlement with you. If at any time you feel that it is not being fair with you or trying to take advantage of you, you may then wish to consult a lawyer.

The reason that good insurance companies will do everything possible to be fair with you is that they know from past experience that with litigation they may have to pay more in handling the claim (even though you yourself may not receive any more than they first offered) and that considerably more work on the part of their personnel may be required, as well as the cost of obtaining the services of defense counsel.

In many instances, the insurance company will have a problem determining who is at fault in the accident. It may be clearly the fault of the company's own assured, but you may have contributed to cause your own injuries. If so, under the law of many states you would then not be entitled to collect. In some states, called *Comparative-negligence states,* you would be entitled to collect, provided your negligence is less than that of the insurance company's assured.

If fault is not clear, the insurance company still may be willing to make some sort of settlement, taking into consideration that either their assured's fault is questionable or your own contributory negligence is also questionable. This means that while they may be willing to pay for your injury, the settlement will be less than otherwise.

You are the person who has to be satisfied. If the insurance company's offer is satisfactory to you, then you may find it desirable to accept the proposed settlement and sign the necessary release.

If you question the amount, and the insurance adjuster is

unable to satisfy you, you may then wish to consult a lawyer. You can accomplish this in two ways. Either you can *retain a lawyer to handle your claim in its entirety* or you can merely *consult him for his advice.* His advice may concern not only the value of injury but also the question of liability (whose fault legally).

If you consult an attorney only to seek his advice, you will have to pay him for the time involved in advising you and for any additional services required. He may find that investigation is needed to give you a good answer. He may have to send investigators out to obtain the needed facts. He may have to obtain your hospital records, as well as an opinion from your doctors as to the nature of your injuries and prognosis. He might have to contact your employer to determine your wage loss.

If you have secured the services of a lawyer whose credentials indicate that he is skilled in handling personal injury claims, he may be able to tell you what your claim is worth. If you are seriously injured or involved in a fault situation that the lawyer does not encounter often, he consults an actuarial guide, such as the *Personal Injury Valuation Handbooks,* that tells him what jurors have recently awarded for similar injuries and the chances of winning the case. If you have any question as to how he arrived at his evaluation, ask him if you can see some of his research figures.

You may have read in your newspaper about a large verdict that you believe may indicate that your particular claim is worth a lot of money. It could be true. However, bear in mind that only large verdicts are in the news. In many situations when jurors give claimants nothing or only a very small amount, the results are not usually reported in the newspaper. Your neighbors and friends may tell you about a large settlement that they received. Such statements can be misleading. Your attorney is a much more reliable guide concerning evaluation of a claim than are newspaper articles or the advice of neighbors.

A third way in which attorneys may be retained is on the basis that they will receive a fee only for the amount that they obtain for you over and above the amount offered by the insurance company. Although many attorneys do not like such an arrangement, if the amount you have been offered is grossly inadequate, very few attorneys will refuse to take the case. On the other hand, if the amount that you have been offered is close to the maximum amount, very few attorneys would care to accept the case on this basis. This then gives you a basis to determine whether, in the final analysis, you need an attorney to handle your case.

Your options, in summary, are these.

1. You may be satisfied with the offer of the insurance company and accept it.
2. You may wish to hire a lawyer to handle your case in its entirety.
3. You may consult with a lawyer for his advice only (and may or may not hire him to handle your case).
4. You may retain an attorney to handle your case at a fee based on what he can secure over and above the insurance company's offer.

PRODUCT LIABILITY

There may be instances when you are injured, perhaps as a result of a product, in which you do not know whether you have a valid legal claim or against whom you have a valid claim. Naturally, since the insurance carrier of the manufacturer of the product that may be at fault does not know about the accident, no investigator will be out to see you. In such event you may consider it advisable to consult an attorney to find out if you do have a valid claim and if so, against whom.

ADVANCE PAYMENT FOR INJURIES

If you are seriously injured, require extensive medical treatment, and may lose substantial time from your employment, many insurance companies will pay your expenses, including compensation for your loss of earnings, without requiring you to sign any release or even requiring you to agree on what you will settle for. Naturally, an insurance company won't do this unless it believes there is good likelihood that its insured is at fault. Many insurance companies may even go further. They will recommend and assist you to obtain the best medical treatment possible. The reason is very simple. The sooner you are restored to employment, the smaller the loss will be, and the less the amount that they will have to pay. It is, of course, to your advantage to be restored to health as quickly as possible and to minimize your expenses.

At a later date the insurance adjuster will confer with you concerning settlement. The insurance company will be entitled, of course, to offset the amount that has been paid against any settlement (or any judgment against their assured, in the event you do not settle and decide to go to trial).

PRIOR INJURIES

When you are asked by the insurance investigator whether you had previously been injured, your answer should be truthful. In the first place, if a prior condition caused by a prior injury is aggravated (made worse), you are still entitled to compensation. Aggravation of a previously sustained injury may be as serious and thus worth as much in the eyes of a jury (or perhaps worth more or less), as the original injury. Equally important, most injuries caused by accident and most claims made are reported to a central clearinghouse. Insurance companies maintain such a clearinghouse to prevent more than one claim being made for the same injury. This organization is sometimes referred to as *The Index Bureau.* Therefore, if you have had any other accident and it was reported to an insurance company, or if you have previously made a claim against an insurance company, chances are these facts will be picked up by the insurance carrier during investigation of your latest accident. The procedure followed is this: when setting up a "claim file," the insurance company checks The Index Bureau to see if you have had other accidents and other claimed injuries. Accordingly, if you are not truthful about revealing that you have had a prior injury, this could defeat a meritorious claim that you may wish to make.

Can You Afford a Lawyer?

14

This section could have been entitled: "Can You Afford *Not* to Have a Lawyer?" The most expensive legal service you can get, the most costly, is when you are trying to fend for yourself in an unfamiliar legal situation, particularly if it involves a lot of money. Keep this in mind when deciding whether or not legal services are affordable.

Most legal services are really inexpensive. It is a myth that the average person cannot afford a lawyer. A consultation with a lawyer is like a visit to a doctor's office. In your first consultation you are charged only for professional advice.

Many lawyers will not even charge you for an initial consultation. If the purpose of the consultation is to determine if you have a legal claim against someone, it is quite common for no consultation fee to be charged. For example, you were injured under circumstances that you believe entitles you to compensation. If the lawyer you consulted is of the opinion that you may have a valid claim against someone collectible (or insured), he expects that you will retain him to handle the matter. Consultation fees by lawyers who serve the public are generally low, ranging from $10. The reason for the low consultation fee or no fee at all is that the lawyer wants your future legal business. Lawyers with outstanding skills and those who serve business often charge much higher consultation fees. Bar Association referral plans usually limit the lawyer to a small fee, frequently $10.00 for the initial consultation.

A consultation for a small fee can avoid big legal fees later. Legal problems may be avoided entirely by taking advice early.

LEGAL COSTS MAY BE PAID BY OTHERS

It's true that some lawyers charge very high fees. Big businesses, for example, have intricate legal problems that require lawyers of great technical skill and experience. Their fees are high, lots of time is involved, and the bills are very large.

The average person involved in expensive legal proceedings often finds that the entire cost is paid by someone else. For example, suppose you have an automobile accident and are sued by someone who claims that he was injured by your negligent driving. The legal fees may be very costly, but the insurance carrier of your automobile policy will pay these fees.

Another group of expensive legal services that you don't really have to pay for are those that are paid out of *recovery* (the amount paid to you as a result of legal action). For example, suppose you have been injured in an automobile accident as a result of someone else's carelessness. To get the money due you, you secure the services of a lawyer. The lawyer's fee is paid out of your settlement or verdict. If there is no settlement or no recovery through a verdict, the lawyer usually does not charge you anything for his time, a figure that often can be enormous. The reason he can do this is that he expects the fees earned in similar cases to cover the time he spent on cases for which he did not get paid.

FIND OUT WHAT THE FEES WILL BE

There are legal matters that could result in substantial fees. You can generally find out what legal services will cost or at least get a good estimate. If what you are considering doing is of less value to you than the legal fees involved, then you might as well forget about it. But don't draw a conclusion about the worth of a legal matter until after you've talked with a lawyer and he has given you an estimate of the fee involved.

Many lawyer fees mount up as a result of your own actions.

Suppose you and your spouse don't get along. You are sued for divorce. You are infuriated. Accordingly, you contest the divorce, and you throw every possible roadblock into the proceedings, notwithstanding your lawyer's advice that such conduct will be futile and expensive. Finally, after months (and perhaps years) of the expensive legal maneuvering you have demanded, you at last consent to a divorce. In the meantime you have run up a very large legal bill, and so has your spouse. In such a case, you can't blame the lawyers for the size of the bill and you can't say that lawyers are expensive and not affordable. All your lawyer was doing was trying to carry out your wishes.

A great many legal problems involve property. In matters involving property, a lawyer can often save you many times his legal fee. In cases involving substantial property, you can't afford *not* to see a lawyer. If you have the idea that lawyers are expensive, you may lose valuable legal rights.

Extralegal rights may be involved, rights other than those involving property. Many of your rights cannot be measured in terms of dollars. They involve your person, your freedom, your future. Again you must ask yourself, "how important are these personal rights to me?" You then ask your lawyer for and get an estimate of the fee. The decision is then yours. You will have to decide whether these rights are more important than the fees that will be charged.

If the lawyer you are considering does not list his (or her) fee, and if you are interested in a consultation, telephone the lawyer's office, tell him that you are interested in a consultation, and ask what, if any, charge there will be.

You will be asked what the matter concerns, and you should be prepared to mention very briefly what it is all about. This will assist the lawyer to determine whether or not he is competent to take care of your matter or if he can do so from the standpoint of his time commitments.

THE LAWYER MAY ASK FOR A RETAINER

Unless you are an established client (often, even if you are) a lawyer will ask you for what is often termed a *retainer*. A retainer is an advance of money to cover out-of-pocket expenses, such as deposits on court costs, long-distance calls, copying charges, depositions, and perhaps his legal fee. If you are charged on an hourly basis and you are not a regular client, you will most likely be asked to make a deposit toward your fee.

This is *your money* and is only paid to the attorney to insure that he has a fund of money on hand to take care of his fees when and if he has rendered services on your behalf. He will deposit these funds in a trust account. When he has rendered services on your behalf, he is then entitled to transfer appropriate amounts from the trust account to his regular account.

WHEN YOU CANNOT AFFORD A LAWYER

Legal Aid Societies

Where you have a legal problem but do not have the financial means to engage a lawyer, a Legal Aid Society may be the answer. In various sections of the country the society may have other names, such as Legal Services Society. Legal Aid Societies are quite generally available throughout the country. These are largely funded by the U.S. government through the Legal Services Corporation. In some localities they also receive funds from foundations and community or united funds. They may consist of one or many lawyers—in some cities as many as 30 or even more.

To be eligible for assistance you must have less disposable income than the state minimum. For example, in one large city to be eligible for services a family of four must earn less than $5800 a year. Other societies have different minimum requirements. If the matter is fee generating—such as personal injury— a Legal Aid Society cannot handle your matter. In such kinds of legal matters you should have no trouble engaging a lawyer on a contingent basis—providing you have a good case.

Pro Bono Services

Many attorneys and firms, including some of the largest in the country, will handle without charge legal matters referred by Legal Aid. Some of these may be conflict-of-interest matters, others may be referred because Legal Aid does not have suitable facilities. Some large firms even furnish one or two lawyers on a no-charge basis to Legal Aid.

Law School Legal Clinics

An increasing number of law schools across the country have (where permitted by the state lawyers' licensing authority) a program of legal aid for those without sufficient means. Usually senior students under the supervision of law instructors and, sometimes, other lawyers, will represent you in court or render other services. Check your telephone book for such services.

You've determined that you probably need a lawyer, and you've decided that you at least need a consultation. The next question is: How do I pick a good one?

The Differences among Lawyers

15

Lawyers are people—they come in all sizes, shapes, and varieties. They differ in ability, proficiency, attitudes, work habits, ethics, and efficiency. Each lawyer has his own reputation. If you are aware of this individuality among members of the profession, you will have a better chance of making an intelligent choice.

A large number of lawyers actually specialize, which means that they concentrate or limit their practice to one field of law or a few related fields. Generally, they cannot hold themselves out to the public as "specializing" except in a very few fields of law. As a rule, they can tell the public that they concentrate or practice in a field of law. In some states, such as Ohio, they can only tell the public they are available in certain fields of law.

Most lawyers are oriented toward serving the general public. These include the general practitioners—the lawyers who will assist you with most common legal problems. Other lawyers are oriented toward business. They serve corporations, institutions, and governments (local, state, and federal). Some lawyers serve both the public and business equally well.

There are lawyers who are so well organized that they can accomplish a great deal of law work in very little time. Thus, they may be both proficient and unusually reasonable in their charges. Some lawyers, on the other hand, may give your problem neither prompt nor competent attention. This may be because they are too busy, inefficient, in ill health, too old, alcoholic, or because they simply have bad work habits.

Because of their outstanding skill and reputation and the consequent high demand for their services, some lawyers will charge far more than other lawyers rendering similar services. Some lawyers, for opposite reasons, may charge far less.

Some lawyers, perfectly competent in one field of law, may undertake your problem, even though it is in a field in which they lack competence. Some honestly do the best they can with limited legal skill and knowledge in the field of your problem (and the solution may not turn out very well for you). Others, when faced with a problem in an area in which they are not familiar, will spend all the time necessary to do a competent job. This extra time creates a problem because charges often are based on time. Because of the extra research time needed to bridge their lack of knowledge, they may have to charge more than a lawyer who practices in the problem area. Many lawyers will simply absorb the extra time by not charging you for it.

Lawyers vary greatly in courtroom skills. A small number of lawyers are highly effective in the courtroom. A larger number are merely competent. Too few of the lawyers who appear before our courts are competent in the courtroom, according to Chief Justice Burger of the U.S. Supreme Court.

Some lawyers are effective in dealing with government bureaus. Some are effective negotiators. Still others are especially skilled at drawing complicated documents and handling complicated legal matters.

Some lawyers are proficient in foreign languages. Some have special skills, such as engineering, aviation, business, to mention a few.

COMPETENCE IS THE KEY

When you choose a lawyer you are looking for competence. Competence may be built on the lawyer's education. Some lawyers were graduated with distinction from topflight law schools. Others barely made it through second-rate law schools. Regardless of the excellence of a lawyer's education, unless he keeps up with new legal developments his competence may leave him.

Many lawyers keep up with the significant developments in the law in general. Others keep up to date in one or a few fields of law. Some lawyers (too many, unfortunately) don't even bother to keep up with current court decisions in their own jurisdiction.

It is a difficult task to keep up with legal developments in even one field of law. The reason is this: Congress, state legislatures, municipalities, and government bureaus turn out thousands of new laws and regulations every year. The courts in interpreting these laws and regulations turn out a similar number of written decisions that may be of importance in any number of situations. *It is impossible for a lawyer to keep up with ALL of these developments.* However, lawyers who concentrate their practice on a single segment of the law can (and often do, conscientiously) keep up with the new developments in their field.

It adds up to this: All lawyers are different; a highly skilled practitioner in one field may be incompetent in others. A few lawyers can handle most matters well; others can do only a few things well. Still others can do only a mediocre or even a poor job with any legal problem they try to handle.

YOUTH v. AGE

As a group, the young lawyers of today are more highly qualified than the young lawyers of years ago. Not too many years ago any person who wished to go to law school was admitted to some law school. Only one out of four persons who take the law school admission test today are admitted to law school. Admission is (partially) based on the admission test scores, on the quality of the college attended, and on the standing of the candidate in his college class. This means that the academic qualifications are much higher today than for those who attended law school in the past. In addition, the law schools with a better grade of students have increased their requirements for graduation. Accordingly, the recent graduates of law school are of very high caliber. One must always consider that a young person can devote more energy to the task. Very important to a client who is cost-conscious, a young lawyer will generally work for much less money.

The older lawyer, of course, has the advantage of experience. The quality of his experience is the key. However, for some it is nothing more than making the same mistakes over and over, year after year. The fact that the lawyer is older doesn't necessarily mean that he is more competent. More important, what has he accomplished in law? Has he written law articles, has he been called on by fellow lawyers to instruct them, to serve on bar committees? These are the earmarks of outstanding lawyers. Of course, many fine lawyers do not have any *obvious* accomplishment in the law, and this makes their identification difficult.

The older lawyer naturally brings more experience to the job, but often he has slowed down because of age and ill health. However, in many situations he can accomplish results that are beyond the younger lawyer. This is particularly true with a lawyer who knows influential people and who employs the successful techniques he has developed and the procedures that he has learned over the years. Your question, regardless of age, is this: "Is the lawyer competent to handle my problem to my satisfaction?"

What Kind of Lawyer Do You Need?

16

Before starting to look for a lawyer, ask yourself two questions. (1) What is the *purpose* of the legal service I desire; what do I wish to accomplish? (2) How important is it? Generally, you should look for a lawyer who practices in the field of law in which your problem lies. Then select a lawyer who can accomplish your needs at the lowest cost.

If you are owed $2000 and you want to collect it, you shouldn't seek the services of a lawyer you know who happens to be a trial lawyer. His skill is in a different field. If he accepts the collection assignment as a personal favor to you, he may not be equipped to do a good job. *You need an aggressive collection lawyer.* You should start your search under "Collection Lawyers." If your problem is not very important to you but does require the services of a lawyer, you will undoubtedly save money by employing a lawyer fresh out of law school. What he lacks in experience he may more than make up for by his industry. He will give the matter prompt attention. Your unimportant matter may be an important matter to him.

SPECIALTIES AND FIELDS OF LAW

Law covers the entire range of human activity. To cover this multitude of human activities, including business and government, many, many laws have been enacted, resulting in a vast universe of law. To cope with literally tons of written laws, the legal profession has divided law into numerous *fields of law* and *specialties*. The Standing Committee on Law Lists of the American Bar Association (which recently was disbanded) recognized 158 different fields of law and specialties.

Within the profession for years we have often referred to lawyers who concentrate their practice in a particular field of law as "specializing" in that field of law. To the public, the profession acts as though the legal profession only has two groups of lawyers who can be called "specialists." The first are lawyers who have *historically* been regarded as specialists. (This includes lawyers who deal with patent, trademark, and copyright law, and those who deal with admiralty law.) In recent years some states have been experimenting with the designation or certification of lawyers as specialists in certain fields of law. These lawyers make up the second group of specialists.

In those states that are experimenting with the selection or designation of specialists, the approach differs. Some lawyers have been designated as specialists in a field of law as a result of taking and passing written examinations. They are usually referred to as *certified* in a specialty. Other lawyers (also referred to as certified) have been designated *specialists* in certain fields by virtue of their long experience and reputation in a field of law.

Other states allow a lawyer to *designate* up to three fields of law, regardless of his experience or knowledge. Such a lawyer is allowed to tell the public that he is *designated* in such fields of law. What this amounts to is that he is available to practice in such fields of law and that these are the fields of law that he likes best. But you don't know whether he is qualified in it or merely hopes to become qualified. The idea appears to be that in time the lawyer *designated* will become a lawyer *certified as a specialist*.

Inasmuch as the lawyer-licensing authority in most states has under consideration either the designation or certification of specialists, some states forbid a lawyer to even claim to the public that he or she concentrates his practice in a field of law. This prohibition is strange because the fact may be that he does so concentrate his practice. (It is even stranger when such reference has been permitted for many years by the profession.) Such states now require that the lawyer can only state that he is "available to practice in the field of law." This rule gives the public less information than they had in the past. There is a great deal of doubt that the lawyer-licensing authorities can legally make lawyers conform to this regulation. The Supreme Court of the United States, ruling in *Bates v. State Bar of Arizona* (in effect, authorizing advertising by lawyers), indicated that the purpose is to enable lawyers to give the public more information about their qualifications so that the public can make an intelligent choice of counsel. You may find that notwithstanding prohibitions by lawyer-licensing boards (often the Supreme Court of the state), lawyers may still refer to themselves as "concentrating their practice in a field of law."

158 FIELDS OF LAW

There is a considerable amount of overlapping in the 158 fields of law that have been designated by the former Standing Committee on Law Lists of the American Bar Association. Some legal matters properly fall within more than one field of law. For example, a claim for personal injury as a result of an automobile accident may fall within the following fields of law: personal injury law, automobile law, general negligence trials and appeals, negligence law, tort law, product liability law, trial practice, and general practice law. A lawyer practicing in any of these fields may be competent to handle your personal injury case.

Many fields of law are so narrow and so often related to others that many lawyers who concentrate their practice in a narrow segment of the law may actually be practicing in several different fields of law. For example, a lawyer who professes to specialize in the field of divorce law also practices in family law, and a lawyer classified under business law also practices corporation law.

All of the different fields of law may not be represented by lawyers in all localities. Some are not available because there is no need in the area (for example, mining law in a nonmining area); others because there are few lawyers practicing this particular specialty and none are available in the particular area, examples being space law and computer law. If you have need of a lawyer in a certain field of law and one is not available in your locality, you can locate lawyers in this field by referring to the *Lawyer's Register by Specialties and Fields of Law.* A list of directories that will help you locate the lawyer you need is shown in Chapter 22. Your lawyer also has another directory available to assist him in locating a lawyer with special skills, the *Lawyer-to-Lawyer Consultation Panel* Directory.

Here are the 158 fields of law presently recognized.

Accident & Health Insurance Law
Administrative Law
Admiralty Law
Adoption Law
Advisor on Laws of (foreign country)
Agricultural Law
Aircraft Title Law
Antitrust Law
Appellate Practice
Arbitration Law
Atomic Energy Law
Attorney-Adjuster Claims
   Investigations & Adjusting
Automobile Law
Aviation Law
Banking Law
Bankruptcy Law
Business Law
Casualty Insurance Law
Cemetery Law
Chancery Practice
Civil Practice
Civil Rights Law
Civil Service Law
Collection Law
College Law
Commercial Law
Commodities Law
Communications Law
Computer Law
Condemnation Law
Condominium Law
Constitutional Law
Construction Law
Consumer Law
Contract Law
Cooperative Law

Copyright Law
Corporate Financing Law
Corporation Law
Creditors Rights Law
Criminal Law
Custody Law
Customs Law
Divorce Law
Drainage & Levee Law
Election Law
Eminent Domain Law
Employee Benefit Law
Energy Law
Entertainment Law
Environmental Law
Equal Opportunity Law
Equity Practice
Estate Planning
Family Law
Federal Employers Liability Law
Federal Excise Tax Law
Federal Gas Law
Federal Income, Estate &
   Gift Tax Law
Federal Power Law
Federal Practice
Fidelity & Surety Law
Fire Insurance Law
Food & Drug & Cosmetic Law
Foreign Patent Law
Franchise Law
General Negligence Trial & Appeals
General Practice
Government (or Public) Contract Law
Health Care & Hospital Law
Housing & Urban Development Law
Immigration & Nationality Law

Indian Affairs Law
Insolvency Law
Insurance Law
International Business Law
International Law
Interstate Commerce Law
Interstate Land Sales Law
Invasion of Privacy Law
Juvenile Law
Labor Law
Landlord & Tenant Law
Legal Affects, & Discipline Law
Legislative Practice
Libel & Slander Law
Licensing Law
Life Insurance Law
Literary Property Law
Litigation
Livestock Law
Local Practice (Washington, DC only)
Malpractice Law
Marine & Inland Marine Insurance
  Law
Maritime Law
Maritime Negligence Law
Medical Legal Law
Mental Health Law
Military Law
Mining Law
Mortgage Law
Motion Picture Law
Motor Carrier Law
Municipal Bond Law
Municipal Finance Law
Municipal Law
Natural Resources Law
Negligence Law
Nuclear (or Atomic) Law
Oil & Gas Law
Partnership Law
Patent Law
Patent, Trademark & Copyright Law
Pension & Profit Sharing Law
Personal Injury Law
Petroleum Law

Poverty Law
Probate Law
Products Liability Law
Public Authority Financing Law
Public Employment Relations Law
Public Housing Law
Public Improvement Law
Public Land Law
Radio Law
Railroad Law
Real Estate Law
Reorganization Law
Savings & Loan Law
School Law
Securities Law
Selective Service Law
Shopping Center Law
Social Security Disability Law
Space Law
Sports Law
State & Local Tax Law
Steamship Law
Subrogation Law
Surety Law
Taxation Law
Television Law
Theatre Law
Timber & Logging/Lumber Law
Tort Law
Trademark Law
Trade Regulation Law
Transportation Law
Trial Practice
Trust Law
Unfair Competition Law
University Law
Urban Affairs Law
Utility Law
Veterans Law
Wage & Hour Law
Water Rights Law
Workmen's (or Workers')
  Compensation Law
Zoning Law

GENERAL PRACTITIONERS

If you have any doubt about the nature of your legal problem, you had best start with a general practitioner. Most general practitioners are equipped to handle common personal legal problems. This includes divorces, wills, simple agreements, and deeds, to mention only a few. If the general practitioner is conscientious and your problem is outside the area of his competence, he should and probably will refer you to a lawyer who is competent, or he will associate himself with such a lawyer. The cost to you may be the same as if you had originally secured the services of the second lawyer.

Selecting a Lawyer

17

By this time you have decided whether to retain a lawyer to handle your problem for you or to take a chance on handling the problem yourself. If you've decided to hire a lawyer, you probably know what type of lawyer you want, whether you want a specialist or a general practitioner, and are sure that you can afford to have a lawyer. Now the question is, "How do I go about finding a good lawyer that I'll want to work with?"

RECOMMENDATIONS OF RELATIVES AND FRIENDS

Your friends, relatives, and business associates may offer to recommend a lawyer to you. This is a good place to start in the selection process. The only thing that you really know at this point is that they are "recommending" him.

Before you give such recommendations any weight, you should consider whether your friends would know a good lawyer from a bad one. Also you should determine whether they are disinterested. (For example, the recommendation of a lawyer by a relative may be on a basis other than merit.) Did the person making the recommendation have sufficient contact with the lawyer to be able to judge his capabilities?

What, if anything, did the lawyer do for the person? Was it similar or related to your problem? For example, the recommended lawyer may have handled the legal work for the purchase of a house. Your problem may be to secure compensation for personal injury. A good real estate lawyer may not necessarily be a good personal injury lawyer.

If the recommended lawyer has done considerable work over long periods of time for the person who recommends him, you can give the recommendation weight, provided the services rendered are relevant to your problem. Satisfaction on the part of a client is not necessarily a guarantee that the lawyer's services were really excellent. It is not unusual for a lawyer with a good "bedside manner" to render substandard legal work and still have more legal work than he can handle.

CONSIDER HIS CREDENTIALS AND EXPERIENCE

Securing information about your prospective lawyer is a very important part of the selection process. Information about lawyers is available from many sources. Lawyer directories, referred to as *law lists,* can be helpful. See chapter 22 for the names of the many law lists that may be available to you at your public library. If you are considering lawyers that are listed in a directory, look to see what information is given besides name, phone number, address, and law firm. You may find enough information in it to make an intelligent choice. Information about a lawyer's experience can also be secured from clients, friends, and your business associates. A good source of information is the lawyer himself. You may have to question him about his legal experience. You have a right to ask him.

Some lawyers develop aptitude, knowledge, and skills in certain fields as the years go by. Others, sad to relate, develop little knowledge and aptitude in any field. Some lawyers read avidly, study, and keep up with new developments in law and their special fields of law. Others do not keep up with the times. Some lawyers develop great competency. Others, unfortunately, do not. A few are relatively incompetent or, at best, merely fair. They may even be poor in their profession. Judging by past standards, many lawyers were acceptable in the past, but by today's greater requirements of legal knowledge and skill they are not. This means that a lawyer who has served you adequately in the past may, by today's superior standards, be substandard. If superior competency is desired, you may wish to consider other counsel.

In most states there is a provision of the Code of Professional Responsibility that sets forth a requirement of competency. It reads as follows:

> A lawyer shall not handle a matter unless he is competent to do so, unless he associates with a lawyer who is.

Unfortunately, the lawyer himself is the judge as to whether he is competent to handle a legal matter. Further, this is a relatively new ethical provision, and it is presently almost never enforced. It could become of importance, however, in cases where a lawyer undertakes a legal task for which he is not competent, raising a question of legal malpractice.

It is easier to find out which lawyers are above average in skills and experience than it is to locate incompetents. It should be pointed out that a lawyer who is brilliant in one field may be inadequate or even incompetent in others. A person who is not a good trial lawyer, for example, may be highly competent in many other respects in the practice of law.

Chief Justice Burger of the United States Supreme Court recently criticized the competence of trial lawyers. Yet his own competency may be questioned. In a recent survey among trial lawyers and scholars of legal systems, Chief Justice Burger was placed at the bottom of the scale among members of the U.S. Supreme Court in a rating of competency and effectiveness.

JUDGING HIS QUALIFICATIONS

If you have meaningful information about the competency of lawyers in certain fields of law, you can make an intelligent choice, at least to the point of selecting several likely candidates for your final choice of a lawyer.

For many years law lists and directories have been available to enable attorneys to select counsel, particularly for areas outside those in which they themselves serve. A corporation, for example, that desires counsel to handle matters in a specific field of law will locate competent lawyers through the lawyers in its legal department, who will consult law lists and the information contained in them about lawyers.

The Lawyer's Register by Specialties and Fields of Law, The Lawyer-to-Lawyer Consultation Panel Directory, and the *Martindale-Hubbell Law Directory* contain meaningful information about lawyers nationally. Other directories and law lists (33 national, 25 state, and 3 foreign) over the past 100 years have been available to members of the bar, government boards, and corporations, such as insurance companies and banks. (See chapter 22 for a complete list of legal directories and where they can be obtained.)

ADVERTISING IS NOW PERMITTED

In evaluating lawyers, it is suggested that you do not eliminate a lawyer from consideration merely because he advertises. Advertising by lawyers is now permitted by a U.S. Supreme Court ruling. Advertising by lawyers is important to the public in that a greater fund of information about lawyers thus becomes available. If the lawyer furnishes little or no information about his background and qualifications, you would be smart to avoid selecting that lawyer. Information is needed to enable you to make an intelligent choice. When you look at a lawyer's advertising, look to see what information he gives you that will help you determine his competency. He may not have the qualifications you are looking for.

The guidelines for lawyers' advertising require that such advertising must be truthful. A lawyer isn't allowed to say laudatory things about himself, but he can state facts about his background, education, experience, professional membership, published works, honors, and activites—all of which can assist you in judging whether he is likely to be competent in handling your legal problem.

GUIDELINES TO AID YOUR SELECTION

1. *Is the lawyer recognized by the rest of the profession as being unusually proficient in a field of law?* Lawyers judge one another. You can determine what lawyers think of the lawyer you have in mind by his selection to hold office, to teach, and to lead other lawyers in legal organizations.

Generally lawyers who have better-than-average proficiency in the field are selected to be on the law committees of bar associations. Even better credentials are indicated if the lawyer is selected as chairman of a bar committee in a particular field of law. Chairmanship indicates that his fellow lawyers consider him outstanding. Otherwise, they would not have selected him to chair such a committee.

The best indication of the proficiency of a lawyer in a field of law is his selection to speak and to teach other lawyers at legal seminars. Such speakers and teachers are recognized by the profession as being unusually proficient. Lawyers who are asked to write articles for law reviews and legal periodicals and who author legal books are likewise recognized for their outstanding proficiency.

2. *Does he belong to professional associations?* Membership in professional associations indicates an active interest in maintaining high professional standards.

The most important bar association from the standpoint of proficiency is the American Bar Association. The American Bar Association is divided into many law sections, such as Family Law, General Practice, Real Property and Probate and Trust Law, Taxation, and Criminal Justice, to mention a few. The sections, in turn, are divided into numerous committees dedicated to assisting the public and educating the members of the profession to do a better job for their clients. For example, the Family Law section is divided into what are called substantive law committees, some of which are adoption, alimony, maintenance and support, bill of rights for children, custody, divorce law and procedures, juvenile justice, legal problems of the aging, marriage, and family counseling. All of the 158 different fields of law are covered by at least one American Bar Association Committee. To give you an idea of the extent of the numerous committees of the ABA, a 353-page directory is necessary to list just the officers, committee chairmen, and vice chairmen.

The most proficient lawyers attend the meetings of the American Bar Association and consequently tend to be most active within the organization. Those recognized by other lawyers for proficiency are often named to committee membership and may rise to vice chairmanship and chairmanship of a law committee. This almost invariably means that such a lawyer is nationally outstanding. These membership credentials are of importance. Lawyers who have attained them list these chairmanship honors in their credentials.

3. *Is he active in bar activites?* Active participation in bar activities often indicates an efficient, proficient practicing lawyer.

In the profession it is said that if you want something done, get a busy lawyer. A lawyer who has attained prominence in a field of law among his fellow lawyers and who attains leadership positions in bar associations demonstrates considerable energy and efficiency and gets things done. Writing, active participation in bar association activities, speaking, and teaching at seminars generally do not appear to interfere with the lawyer's practice. Surprisingly, such active leaders in the profession are very attentive to the work of their clients and produce a surprisingly high volume of high-grade legal work. Of course, such a lawyer probably works on Saturdays and Sundays and from early morning into the night—but this is the penalty of leadership in this profession as in most others. (Activity of itself means little without accomplishment. Some lawyers who appear to be very busy create such an impression through inefficiency or improper management of their staff, and often cannot take care of their work promptly.)

4. *What is his legal experience?* Pertinent experience is important. If your problem lies with the government or a bureau of the government, you should consider hiring a lawyer who has had government experience in the area of your problem. For example, if you have a tax problem with the Internal

Revenue Service, you could seek a lawyer who is now in private practice of law but who was formerly with the IRS. Such a person would know a lot more about handling your income tax matter, and if a controversy should occur, such a lawyer would know the ins and outs and might even know the personnel at the bureau—all of which could help you get a good result. If you have a matter involving the Industrial Commission, a lawyer who has worked with the Industrial Commission would be of interest to you. Try to find a lawyer with experience in the area of your problem.

5. *What are his legal education and scholastic honors?* Particularly if you are considering a young lawyer, it is important to find out which law school he has attended and whether the lawyer received any scholastic honors or distinctions. Such honors are indications of excellence and application. For example, an important scholastic distinction is to be on the law review, and even more so, to be editor of the law review. Another is to be elected to the "Order of the Coif." This is a national law student honor society.

The quality of law schools varies. A school noted for its high standards and requirements reflects on the merits of its graduates. For example, it is recognized that a graduate of Harvard, Michigan, Stanford, or University of Chicago law schools (to mention only a few of the top law schools) has met very high standards to enter law school as well as to graduate from it. However, many fine lawyers graduated from lesser law schools (including "night law schools"), even those that do not meet the ABA standards.

6. *What courts and boards has he been admitted to or has he served on?* If you have a matter before courts or various boards you should determine what courts and boards the lawyer has been admitted to and the relevancy to your problem. For example, if you have an important income tax problem that may go to the tax court, you should secure an attorney who is admitted to practice before it. Likewise, if your problem involves zoning, a former member of the zoning board may be able to secure better results for you.

To get permission from a government agency to do something, such as to start a truck route, various procedures often are required. These may require formal hearings and decisions by a board or a government bureau. Often, to get the desired result, an appeal to a court may be necessary. Practice before government agencies and boards often requires considerable specialized knowledge to be able to cope with the red tape and procedures involved. Accordingly, it becomes highly desirable to retain a lawyer who is familiar with the governmental agency.

7. *Has he held public or quasi-public offices?* If your problem lies in the political arena, you may find that public office held by the lawyer may assist you in your problem. For example, if he has been mayor of your city, he may know the right people to assist you if your problem involves local political approval. If your lawyer has formerly been a councilman, for example, he will know how to secure building permits and help you cut red tape in getting desired results from the city.

8. *Is he involved in civic activities?* A lawyer's contacts can be of great importance and relevancy. A lawyer who is active in civic activities gets to know the important political and business figures in a community. This often puts him in a position to secure results for you that would not be easily achieved otherwise. He may know people who make the necessary decisions or who can bring pressure upon those who do.

9. *What clients does he represent?* A list of the lawyer's clients can be very helpful. In published biographies, the client list is a very important item. If the lawyer represents people or corporations whom you respect, this may well be an important indication of his competency, particularly if he has handled problems similar to yours for clients similar to you.

10. *What is your personal opinion of the lawyer?* This is an extremely important point. You can't have any personal opinion of a lawyer, of course, until you meet him and talk with him. So you should not (except outside your locality) hire a lawyer unseen. It may be that a telephone contact will help you decide whether you want to see him about a specific problem. But you should not retain a lawyer until after you have talked to him and have decided that he is right for you, that he will do the best job for you at reasonable cost.

The screening process in today's law schools ensures a higher degree of aptitude and intelligence. Persons who have not demonstrated a reasonable ability to learn will not be admitted to law school. Applicants must meet scholastic standards, grades in college have to be good, and response to the law school aptitude test has to meet high standards, otherwise they will not be admitted to law school. Three out of four persons who take the law aptitude test do not get into law school. The school itself applies a further screening process. Only those with aptitude and application make it through school; some students do not graduate.

The bar examinations are the next hurdle for aspiring lawyers who have proved themselves bright and knowledgeable enough to be graduated. The bar examination is a comprehensive test required by most states. The test is very difficult. A bar examination may take a full day, or even several days to complete. If the law graduate does not pass, he will not be admitted to practice.

Today's law school graduates who have passed the state bar examination and become licensed to practice have been well screened, so far as aptitude, intelligence, and *limited* legal knowledge are concerned. (Law schools do not teach all the skills necessary for the competent practice of law. Often missing, among others, is how to skillfully handle a case in court or how to draft a complicated legal document. These skills have to be learned through experience.)

Should I Go to a Law Firm?

18

Although many lawyers are individual practitioners, the majority of lawyers today are affiliated with or are members of law firms, legal associations, and other legal units, such as legal clinics. Your choice of a lawyer may also involve choosing the organization with which he is affiliated. This can be very important to you in securing the best possible legal service.

INDIVIDUAL PRACTITIONERS

Today, fewer than half of the lawyers practicing are individual practitioners. Many are sole practitioners because they like to be independent—to work alone. Some work alone because they can't get along with other lawyers in any form of association.

A lawyer who is in practice alone, a sole practitioner, often shares office space with other lawyers and shares their facilities, such as a law library and office equipment. Being officed together, some sole practitioners may use a firm name. This is often done to give the appearance of an organization of lawyers and to create an impression of greater facilities and more prestige. Often sole practitioners will work together or at least cover for one another with clients and the courts. However, the lawyer may not have a reciprocal arrangement with his associates or he may be in an office by himself.

If you have a problem when your sole practitioner is on vacation or ill, you will have to wait or see another lawyer. You may find it desirable, in case it becomes important to you, to inquire if an associate will take care of you in your own lawyer's absence.

LAW FIRMS

Law firms may consist of any number of lawyers, from two to several hundred. They may have many offices and offices in other states. We expect an evolution in law very soon that will see the rise of law firms that are national—firms with offices in all principal cities. The average size of a law firm today appears to be from five to fifteen lawyers. Many law firms that serve businesses and large corporations are growing very rapidly and are generally larger than those who primarily serve the public. Legal problems of corporations, largely because of increasing regulations, are rapidly multiplying. Regardless of size and whether they are business-oriented or not, most firms will serve members of the public at least in some fields of law.

SIZE CONSIDERATIONS

Most small legal firms are in the general practice of law, which means that they practice in many fields of law. Some firms cover almost all fields. Within the firm, however, one or more of the lawyers may concentrate their practice in a few fields of law. For example, a small firm may have a lawyer who devotes most of his time to real estate, another to family law, a third to small corporations, and a fourth to personal injury practice. Some of the lawyers are partners, others may be lawyer employees.

In some firms all of the lawyers may practice the same field of law or specialty. For example, a firm may "specialize" in patent and copyright law, another in personal injury law. Some small firms may represent mainly corporations and affluent people. Others are oriented toward the general public. Still others have a "mix"—they represent both corporations and the general public. The size of the firm has little to do with general competence, but it does affect the number of different fields of law covered by lawyers who concentrate their practice on one or a few fields of law. Some of the small firms are as productive as a much larger firm because they employ modern technology and are efficiently run, needing only a few lawyers. Such firms often produce high-grade legal service at low cost.

Because they contain more lawyers, medium-sized firms tend to have a greater number of lawyers who specialize in a single field of law than a small firm has. They tend to be more oriented toward serving business than smaller firms. They also tend to avail themselves of modern technology and legal assistants to a greater extent than small firms. A firm of from 15 to 40 lawyers may be called medium-sized.

Large firms, because of the large number of lawyers and employees, are sometimes referred to as "law factories." Very large firms tend to be business-oriented, particularly toward large corporations. The large firms often include many more specialists than are to be found in smaller and medium-sized firms. Because large firms can command very high fees, they often tend to be very conservative. Although they can afford to utilize the maximum in technology, many do not. They may spurn modern technology and the more efficient electronic equipment.

INCORPORATED LAW FIRMS

For tax reasons, firms may incorporate. Pension plans for corporations can be more generous and less costly than for partnerships. However, where the licensing authority of a state permits lawyers to incorporate, they do not allow the lawyer to escape personal liability by its use. This means that a lawyer who is technically an employee of an incorporated law firm may be held liable for the mistakes of an associate just as he would have been held liable for those of a partner. (This is in contrast to an incorporated business outside the legal field. The owner of all the shares of stock of an ordinary corporation will not necessarily be held liable personally for the mistakes of an employee).

LEGAL CLINICS

A relatively new type of organization in the legal field is the *legal clinic*. Such organizations advertise extensively to attract as many clients as possible. The theory behind the legal clinic is to provide legal services in volume; they will accept only routine matters for which costs can be kept down by the use of standardized forms and office procedures. Legal clinics are geared to provide standardized and multiple services on a "production-line" basis. By securing a substantial volume of work that falls within routine categories, they can keep costs down. If you are not concerned with the lack of personal attention and if you are interested only in having your legal matter handled routinely at the lowest possible cost, you may wish to consider a legal clinic.

Unfortunately, some organizations of lawyers call themselves "clinics" when they are not clinics in the true sense of the word but are merely capitalizing on the current popularity of the term. You may find it to your best interest to determine whether the organization is really a clinic or merely one or more lawyers using the term "clinic" as a come-on. You may find it worthwhile to compare their advertised charges with those of another lawyer that you are considering. You may find little or no difference.

FIRMS WITH OTHER OFFICES

The larger the law firm, the greater the potential for proficiency and efficiency. The needs of clients in other localities may dictate the opening of other offices. Naturally, such firms offer facilities over a wider geographic area. If your legal problems require services in other areas, a firm with offices in the desired area should be of interest. Often such a multioffice firm can serve you better than a local firm in another city—your multioffice firm may know what you want, and to them you may be a more important client.

What to Do Before You Go To the Lawyer's Office

19

You have secured information about lawyers who appear to be competent in the field of law you are concerned with. You are now in a position to make a tentative selection of lawyers who you believe can serve you best. If you have more than one lawyer on your list, decide which lawyer you believe will best meet your needs.

The next step is to talk with the lawyer.

Never go to see a lawyer without first calling for an appointment. But, *before you call the lawyer:*

1. Write out a short summary of your problem.
2. Decide if the amount of the consultation fee is important to you.
3. Decide what you will do if you are advised that the lawyer will not be available (due to vacation, extended business, illness) for an extended time. Decide if you will be willing to wait for his return or to be taken care of by an associate (if he has one who is qualified to take care of your problem).

CALLING FOR AN APPOINTMENT

Call the lawyer at his office, never at his home—unless yours is an emergency matter (for example, if you have been arrested and are to be jailed) and you must talk to a lawyer at once.

Ask to speak with the lawyer you have selected. If he is out, ask that he call you back. Ask when he is expected to return. Leave a message that it is a new legal matter that you wish him to handle.

If the lawyer or an associate or his secretary does not call you back within several days of his expected return, you may wish to consider calling the attorney next on your list. The reason: if the first lawyer or his office is not organized to return your call promptly, you can probably expect similar difficulty in the future with this lawyer. Most attorneys—even most of those who are not usually prompt—will promptly return calls of a potential new client.

When you speak to the lawyer, tell him the nature of the problem. For example, that it is a domestic relations problem, personal injury, purchase of a home, etc. Do not go into any detail unless the lawyer asks you to do so. The reason for stating the nature of the problem is that it may turn out to be the kind of legal problem that he does not handle, and he may so advise you. Also, it gives him a better idea as to how much time he should allow for the interview.

Ask the lawyer if there will be a fee for the first appointment. As previously pointed out, some attorneys do not charge for the initial interview or for certain kinds of cases, such as personal injury. If there is a fee, ask how much or the *basis* for the charges. (He may charge on a time basis, perhaps from $10 to $15 for each quarter of an hour.) Most consultation fees are modest, and the lawyer expects payment upon completion of the interview—unless it is clear that further work may be required or that he may be paid out of a settlement or by the opposing side. If the lawyer expects a consultation fee, take along with you sufficient money to cover. Do not set up an appointment if you are not satisfied with the fee arrangement. Likewise, if you don't like the way the lawyer handles himself or his attitude over the telephone, consider the next attorney on your list.

You may have to set up an appointment with the lawyer without first talking to him. He may, for example, be tied up in court but be willing to talk to you after court hours. If the consultation fee amount is important, his secretary can most likely furnish you the necessary information.

PREPARE FOR YOUR FIRST VISIT

Remember, most consultations are on a time basis. If you can furnish your lawyer with the brief details of your problem in writing you can save fee time. A short summary of your problem will do. List the facts in the order that they happened.

Make a special note of all papers or documents that relate to the facts of your problem. Get as many of these papers together as possible and present them to the lawyer at your first appointment.

Allow yourself adequate time to get to your lawyer's office in time. If you are late, you may throw off his schedule—or worse, he may not be able to see you until a later date or time.

Interviewing and Evaluating The Lawyer

20

Except if you are unable to leave your home because of age, injury, or illness, you will go to the lawyer's office. Some lawyers, for other reasons than the above, will be willing to stop at your home or office to talk to you about being retained. When it is possible for you to see the lawyer at his office, do so. Observation of his office, associates, and personnel will tell you a lot about him and them.

You can learn much about a lawyer's competence during an interview, through your personal observation. Especially if you are going to require regular legal service, you should interview the lawyer and take note of his equipment and facilities to determine if he can serve your needs efficiently, promptly, and competitively in price.

FIRST IMPRESSIONS

Location of the Law Office

Location may tell you a great deal about the lawyer. If his office is housed in a dilapidated or second- or third-rate building when better ones are available, you should be suspicious of his abilities. Generally, successful lawyers with good clientele will have offices in the best buildings. This does not necessarily mean the newest building, because location is very often important; and in many cities, old buildings often are considered as desirable and as prestigious as some of the new ones.

The waiting room. What does the waiting room look like? Is it neat or run down? Observe the receptionist and the secretaries that may be visible. Are they neat and businesslike? If the office appears to be in turmoil, you must bear in mind that your work may join the turmoil.

The office. When you are ushered into the lawyer's office, observe it carefully. If it is cluttered, your work may join the clutter. If you note that he appears to lack organization, you should be suspicious. Your case may get lost in the shuffle or it may not be taken care of expeditiously. If you're there to defend yourself from a lawsuit, for example, you must be concerned that he will take care of it within the answer date or get it extended. Unless his office is properly organized, he may overlook a time limitation. A default judgment could be rendered against you. This could be quite costly to you. Equally costly, he may let the statute of limitations expire on your cause of action.

The lawyer's appearance. The lawyer's appearance tells you a great deal about him. Is he neat? Does he dress reasonably well? Does he look like the kind of person that you want to represent you? Appearance is of great importance in trial work. Does your lawyer inspire confidence? Is he believable? Is he sincere?

His speech. His speech will often tell you a good deal. Is he coordinated? Is his speech pleasing? Does he appear to know what he is talking about? Does he have good command of the English language? This is particularly true if you need him to handle a trial or delicate negotiation.

How he handles himself. Does he inspire confidence in you? In discussing your legal matter with him, is he promising you too much? Is he believable? If your matter has questionable chance for success, is he telling you that he will have no problem winning? If you are there because you have been injured and want to see about collecting, is he promising to get you a sum that you know is far too great, considering your injuries?

INTERVIEW THE LAWYER

The lawyer will interview you. Of course, you should also interview him. You must determine if he is the right lawyer for you. In many instances this is not necessary, as you will have sufficient information before you step into his office. However, when the information about him is sketchy and you would like to know more, you should ask questions.

Be prepared to change your mind. Don't hesitate to reject a lawyer if he doesn't measure up to your expectations. If it is apparent to you that the lawyer is not going to be able to help you, that you simply don't think he is competent in the area of your problem, thank him and leave. If you have not addressed yourself to your problem—only to his ability, competence, and facilities to handle your problem or legal work, you probably owe him nothing. If you have asked his advice, then you owe him for the consultation only. Many persons do not know how to say no or how to close an interview. It is simple. Thank the lawyer and leave.

Questions You May Ask—Observations You Should Make

Is the lawyer experienced in the kind of law you require? Perhaps the matter you are consulting him about may lie beyond his particular experience and training or beyond his particular competence in a field of law. If so, would he associate a lawyer with him who is competent? Ask him directly, "Are you experienced in this field?" If you are not satisfied with his answer, you should ask him to state his experience in the written retainer agreement. For example, suppose you are conferring with him and considering retaining him to handle a serious auto accident, which you have reason to believe was caused by a defective automobile. You may wish him to state that he has handled the preparation and trial of product liability claims. He may give you the impression that he is competent. But if you ask him to put a statement of his experience in writing, you have better assurance that his experience is what he says it is.

Does he keep up with the law? You will also want to determine whether he regularly keeps up with new legal developments. Does he read the advance sheets (reports of new court decisions), does he regularly attend legal seminars? What and when was the last seminar he attended? What does he read?

Where relevant, you may wish to see samples of his work. Does he draw any wills or any contracts? If so, ask to see examples. Is the document neat or full of mistakes and badly typed? The appearance of a document is important. Today with modern word-processing equipment, legal documents can be prepared not only to be good but to look good. What does his correspondence look like?

Does he have adequate secretarial facilities? If you see one secretary and five lawyers you know that he has to be doing a lot of things for himself that a secretary could do for him. Are you willing to pay $50 an hour for work of an attorney that he could have had done for $5 an hour by a secretary?

How will he handle your retainer? If he is going to be handling your money—for example, in collections or a substantial retainer—does he put this money in a trust account as he should? You must ask.

Does he have malpractice insurance? Even the best of lawyers can occasionally make a serious mistake that may well be malpractice. Does he have malpractice insurance to protect you if a sizable loss occurs affecting you? You would hate to find out that he doesn't have much in the way of assets. It is not unusual for a lawyer whose office is poorly organized to let the statute of limitations expire, which can result in a great loss to a client. Losses of $100,000 have occurred because of inattention on the part of the lawyer. Recently a sizable and prestigious firm located in a large city apparently mishandled the merger of a number of corporations. The firm's malpractice carrier settled a multimillion dollar judgment for $1.2 million!

Does he have a library available?   What are his facilities? Does he have at least an adequate working library? Does he keep the library up to date? Does his library have the necessary books to help him properly handle the matters you have come to see him about? If he has a specialty, does he have the books that the specialty requires? For example, if he claims he specializes in personal injury, does he have medical books and the Personal Injury Valuation Handbooks available? These handbooks give verdict information for various types of injury cases, depending on the severity, and the chances for a successful verdict in the various fault situations.

If the legal matter involves important questions of law that a lawyer can't be expected to know without research, you may wish to ask him what facilities he has for research. Does he do it himself? Does he have a research clerk who can do the work (at lower cost)? In many rural areas the lawyer may not have many books, but does have available the county law library close by. (If he has to go some distance for research, you may have to pay travel time.) Ask about his law library if you believe it is important.

LAW WORK IS PAPERWORK

Often you have the opportunity of observing office equipment. Is it old? Is it obsolete? Does the lawyer's office employ modern technology—that is, word processors, the latest in electric typewriters, dictaphones, and copying equipment? Is computer technology available? If your matter requires long, complicated legal documents, word-processing equipment is important. If the work that you contemplate requires a lot of typing, obsolete equipment not only will not do as good a job, but considering the necessary revisions, the cost can be considerably higher than through the use of modern *word processors* (computerized typewriters).

By the nature of the work a lawyer's office is essentially a "paper mill" turning out a flood of documents. Lawyers carry on extensive correspondence, prepare briefs, and draw wills, trusts, deeds, and agreements of all kinds—to mention only a few. Many of these legal documents are long and require many pages of typed material. Even the best typists make errors that must be corrected—often requiring entire pages to be retyped. Lawyers often must make extensive revisions to improve documents, to please a client, or to meet the requirements of an opposing attorney.

When using word processors, the operator simply types in the corrections and revisions. Then the typewriter, often at ten times the effective speed of even the best typist, will automatically type an error-free document of many pages. While this is going on, the typist can do other work.

In a law office that is not equipped with a computerized typewriter, the secretary may spend many hours retyping the document. Because the secretary can make errors that were not there before, the lawyer must reread every word again, even the paragraphs that were not corrected or revised. This time is chargeable to you. The secretary may again have to retype pages of the document. It is obvious that if a lawyer does not have available modern word-processing equipment, the cost of preparing letters and documents is much higher in secretary's time and lawyer's time. The final document may not please you because corrected typos may mar the appearance. Since overhead is indicated in the legal fee, lawyers with antiquated equipment must either charge more for their time and their secretary's time or accept less for themselves.

LEGAL ASSISTANTS

Does the lawyer have specially trained assistants to handle aspects of your work that can be handled by them equally as well and at lower costs to you? A well-run office today requires the services of legal assistants. These persons may be "parale-gals": law clerks, docket clerks, and investigators. Paralegals are especially trained to relieve a lawyer of specialized routine tasks that lawyers used to do and, unfortunately, most lawyers still do.

There are many functions within the law office that a paralegal, under the supervision of a lawyer, can accomplish as well as a lawyer but at much lower cost. The result is that a lawyer employing paralegals and other assistants can, and usually does, render topflight legal service more promptly and at lower cost than a lawyer without such assistance. The economics are elementary. Would you use a $40-an-hour lawyer to file papers at the courthouse or to check the docket (as many lawyers still do) when a $10-an-hour docket clerk can do it equally well? Would you use a $50-an-hour lawyer to research law when a $15-an-hour law clerk under the supervision of the lawyer can do a competent job? Would you use a $70-an-hour trial lawyer to arrange for the appearance of witnesses for trial when a paralegal can do it at $20 an hour? Unfortunately, some lawyers even carry out functions that a $5-an-hour secretary can do as well or better.

FEE INFORMATION PRIOR TO EMPLOYING A LAWYER

If you are in the lawyer's office for a consultation, you should already know his consultation fee basis. If not, this is your first question. If not fully satisfied with his response, feel free to thank him and leave.

If you are in his office for legal services, such as handling a divorce, handling your personal injury case, or handling your purchase of a residence, your first question may be what his fee basis is. Also, ask him for an estimate of the probable out-of-pocket expenses that may be incurred in the handling of your matter. This is important in determining whether you wish to go forward with the legal matter, since not only will you be responsible for such expenses but he probably will require you to deposit adequate money in advance of the expenses being incurred.

Out-of-pocket expenses that you may be responsible for include court reporters, photographers, court deposit and/or court costs. Additional expenses for which you may be responsible include services of lawyers from other areas, investigators, and expert witnesses.

For many types of cases, such as representing you in a boundary dispute, in an incorporation, or in a criminal case, your lawyer will ask you for a deposit of money to cover his fee. This is referred to as a *retainer*. Chapter 21 contains more information on fees.

Employing the Lawyer

21

You have decided to retain the lawyer. The first thing you should do is have an understanding of his fee or fee basis *in writing*. The memo should include the amount you are asked to deposit toward expenses and perhaps the fee. This is important, as it not only eliminates misunderstanding but may save you fee dollars. He will dictate a memorandum of retainer setting out what he has undertaken for you and the fee basis. You and the lawyer will sign two copies of this memorandum, and you will be given one copy.

To best understand what fees or fee basis you can expect, we will discuss the way a lawyer works, his fees, and how they are set.

Remember that your lawyer is essentially selling his time (and, of course, his knowledge and skill). A lawyer really has precious little time to sell. A young lawyer may have approximately 2000 hours to sell each year. This may seem like a relatively few hours. However, when you subtract time required to attend legal seminars, to run the office, to consult with associates regarding nonclient matters, and to attend bar and firm meetings, and then add time for such things as vacations and illness, it is a rare lawyer who can devote over 2000 hours a year to clients' work. Many lawyers are lucky to accomplish 1200 client-chargeable hours a year.

HOW A LAWYER WORKS

Unlike, for example, a doctor, a lawyer generally spends very little chargeable time in the client's presence. A lawyer may spend fifteen minutes with the client determining the nature of the client's problem. He may spend hours, days, and sometimes weeks solving it.

For example, suppose you are selling a business that is franchised. You have agreed on the price. You want your lawyer to consummate the sale and draw the necessary agreements. In addition to drawing the documents of agreement, there may be taxes, franchise, and real estate legal problems to solve. Before your lawyer draws the articles of agreement, he has to consider the tax consequences to your best advantage. The savings to you may be considerable. He may spend hours with the Internal Revenue Code and tax court decisions.

He may have to spend considerable time in conference with the other attorney who may, likewise, have tax problem areas to consider. Further, research and conferences may be necessary to iron out the problems. Because the sale involves other fields of law besides taxes, he may have to consult with various associates experienced in franchise law and others experienced in real estate law. Several drafts of a long agreement might be necessary. The other lawyer may insist upon changes in the wording. These may require many hours of his time to best protect your interest.

To represent your best interests, a competent, conscientious lawyer may spend fifteen *minutes* with you and fifteen *hours* outside your presence. A less conscientious or less competent lawyer may not recognize all of the problems and may handle the same transaction in a few hours of time. Although such a lawyer may charge you less for his legal fee, his services can turn out to be very expensive. Unanticipated taxes and problems that could have been avoided may be ten times the original "savings."

THE FEE BASIS

It is important to discuss the fee basis. On some legal matters, when he knows how much time will be required, a lawyer can quote you a definite fee (for example, a will, deed, or an uncontested divorce).

If the employment is on a hourly basis, be sure to ask him his hourly rate. Also find out the hourly rate of any paralegals that he may employ to assist him. Ask him, if possible, to estimate the fee, and find out what, if any, retainer he requires. A retainer is the amount of money that the lawyer needs as an advance toward his fee and his out-of-pocket expenses. If he does not know you, you may be required to give him a retainer unless the lawyer is relying on a recovery to compensate him for his time—as, for example, in a personal injury case. Even for such cases, he may request a retainer to cover out-of-pocket expenses. Find out if he will need refreshers—additional advances against fees and expenses—from time to time. You may ask him about various costs that may be incurred. He is required to deposit your retainer money in a trust account, for the money you gave him as a retainer is yours, less his time and expense charges.

Suppose you engage a lawyer to handle your divorce. He asks for a retainer of $350 toward his fee and $50 for court deposit. This money is then put in a trust account. He then prepares and files on your behalf a divorce petition, depositing $50 with the court as a filing fee. Let us assume that immediately after the filing of the petition for divorce you patch up your differences with your spouse, decide to have your divorce petition dismissed, and call your lawyer and inform him of your desires. Let us assume that he has put in $200 of work up to this point. Assume also that upon dismissal, the court refunds $30 of the court deposit. The lawyer then must refund to you

$180 ($150 remaining deposit toward fees plus the $30 court refund).

Let us assume that instead of dismissing the complaint you desire to go ahead with the divorce. Your lawyer then confers with your spouse's lawyer regarding a separation agreement. This frequently is quite time consuming. He now has rendered an additional $150 worth of services. Your lawyer will then get in touch with you and ask for an additional retainer or, as it is sometimes called, a "refresher."

YOUR LAWYER'S BILL

When a lawyer has rendered services for you on an hourly time basis, upon the completion of the matter he will send you a billing. If the matter he is handling for you is ongoing, he may send you periodic billings. Such bills will consist of the amount of money that you owe him to date for services and other expenditures that he has made on your behalf. Most lawyers will briefly itemize what they have done for you and often will include the amount of lawyer time that was required. Some lawyers will merely send you a bill stating "for services rendered," "for expenses incurred," and the total. If there is any question about this, you are entitled to an itemized bill. Most attorneys will comply with your request.

OFFICE OVERHEAD IS HIGH

Many laymen are of the opinion that lawyers charge too much. This idea is usually based on lack of knowledge of how much lawyer time is required to handle legal problems and how sizable a lawyer's overhead expenses are.

A lawyer must maintain a law office. Most of the services that he renders require considerable paperwork; accordingly, he needs office machines, including typewriters. Because of the long, complicated legal documents often required of the lawyers, and to keep costs down and quality high, he needs a word processor. To operate word processors requires specially trained operators who, because of the skill required, command a large salary—far more than that of an ordinary typist.

Because of the high quality of work necessary in legal documents, legal secretaries have to be among the very best of the secretarial lot. In addition, inasmuch as they deal with highly technical terms that must be spelled correctly and legal formats specified *and required* by the courts, a great deal of training is involved. Accordingly, legal secretaries are among the highest paid in the secretarial field.

LIBRARY NEEDS ARE EXPENSIVE

In addition, to do a good job, your lawyer needs to have a working legal library readily available. These cost a lot of money initially and a great deal more to keep up to date. The courts are grinding out new decisions all the time, and the various government bureaus issue new regulations almost daily. In addition, the lawyer needs to have available all existing law decisions of his state and frequently those of other states and of the United States Federal Courts. The costs are formidable. He may need the regulations and rulings of various government bureaus as well. Court decisions from other state courts may be available in large law libraries. Lawyers have to pay dues and assessments toward the upkeep of those libraries as well as their own.

LEGAL SEMINARS MUST BE ATTENDED

To keep up to date with the latest developments in the law, your lawyer has to attend legal seminars and bar association meetings. These can easily account for several weeks each year and leave him with less actual working time available to devote to the problems of clients than a lawyer has who does not attend these seminars. Yet, it is to your advantage if your lawyer takes time from his practice to attend these. In fact, attending legal seminars is so important that some states require lawyers to attend a certain number each year to continue to qualify to practice law. Other states are considering such requirements. It is just a question of time until most, if not all, states will require that all practicing lawyers engage in continuing legal education.

And That's Not All . . . To protect himself and you, the lawyer needs several kinds of insurance, including malpractice insurance. He has to pay dues to the local, state, and national bar associations, together with sums assessed for a security fund set up for the financial protection of clients.

When added together all these various overhead costs may total $20 to $30 for each hour the lawyer is able to devote to the work of clients. Thus, if he charges you $50 an hour he may have only $20 left for himself.

COMPARE THE COST

An excellent and busy lawyer working long hours often will take home no more money than does a good plumber or an electrician. The difference is that the plumber or the electrician may not have much in the way of overhead. Consequently, if the plumber charges you $20 an hour, almost all of it will be net to him.

The average lawyer takes home about the same amount of money as a middle-management executive. The average lawyer has an income that is approximately one half that of the average medical doctor. The reason that it is difficult for a lawyer to even come close to earning as much as a medical doctor is that the doctor renders his services in your presence. A doctor can spend 5 minutes with you and bill you $15 and you may not be displeased. He may see twelve or more patients in an hour. He may realize $180 an hour, gross.

On the other hand, you may spend an hour with your lawyer telling him about your problem. If he tried to charge you $180 for that hour you would probably storm out of his office and never go back. To make matters even worse for himself, the lawyer may spend 20 hours out of your presence working on your problem. The average client finds it difficult to understand why his lawyer had to spend so much time because the lawyer's services are not rendered in the client's presence.

WHY CORPORATE LAWYERS EARN MORE

When a lawyer works for a large corporation he has less problem about charging for his time because the person who hires him and approves his bill is often a lawyer himself, who understands the time involved and the overhead. Lawyers who have a national reputation and who work on intricate, complicated matters for corporations can charge a great deal for each working hour and take home a substantial amount each year. Such lawyers are the exception in the profession. Some of these lawyers would ordinarily prefer to work for people like you, but so few clients would—even if they could—willingly pay what he is worth and can command from large corporations that he has no real choice.

MUCH FREE TIME IS SPENT IN PUBLIC SERVICE

A lawyer has to be known by the public because public exposure is the means by which he increases his law practice. This is one reason that many lawyers engage in public activities and public service without compensation. As any lawyer's wife will tell you, lawyers get to spend very few evenings at home with their families. In industry the person who sells others his company's product is compensated for his time and will be well compensated if he is successful. A lawyer, if he is lucky, will receive thanks for his public service time but rarely direct compensation. The lawyer often spends considerable time in public service and has expenses that he just can't bill anyone for.

We aren't asking you to feel sorry for lawyers as a class. They chose the profession, and they would not be in any other. Our purpose is to help you understand why your lawyer and the lawyers you know may not have as much money to spend as you do and why.

Because the lawyer often has to spend so much time in working outside the presence of his client, time that is difficult to bill, a problem is created for the client as well as the lawyer. Some lawyers, unfortunately, rather than spend hours on needed legal research, will simply guess at an answer—and they may be wrong, to the client's detriment. Some lawyers try to use shortcuts that are counterproductive to securing the best results.

VARIOUS FEE ARRANGEMENTS

Contingent Fees

A lawyer's fee sometimes depends on the outcome of the legal matter that he is handling. The fee is *contingent* on the outcome of the case. This is commonly used in cases where the lawyer represents a client for personal injuries and is looking to secure a settlement for that client from someone else. The fee arrangement for personal injury generally varies from 25% to 50% of the settlement. This may depend upon the size of the matter and the prospects of recovery of money for you.

Contingent fees sometimes appear to be excessive. You must recognize that when a lawyer handles a matter on a contingent basis, he may spend hundreds of hours on it. If he loses, he will not receive one cent of compensation for his time. The successful cases have to cover those that are not successful. In many instances, liability (legal fault on the part of the defendant) is not at all clear; the lawyer may not be able to afford to represent you unless you agree, for example, upon a 50% basis. On the other hand, if there is a matter that is clear as to fault on the part of the defendant, a 50% fee may be too high. The more likely fee would then be 33-1/3% to 40% unless there are other problems. In addition, costs are involved—filing fees, depositions, photostats, and so forth. Inquire as to what deposit you will have to make for these. Lawyers generally are not permitted by legal ethics to pay these costs, although some may do so anyway.

Fees for Collection Matters

If you are owed money by someone and have to retain a lawyer to collect it, the fee will usually be from 33-1/3% to 50% of the amount collected. You have to advance the court cost deposit. If you are a company that has a volume of claims, the fee may be only 33-1/3% or less.

Set Fee

Set fees are for work that can be estimated—for example, a deed, an uncontested divorce, a simple incorporation.

Hourly Rate

An hourly rate is usually used on matters where the lawyer cannot determine in advance how much time he is going to have to put in to represent you or to handle your legal problem. Hourly rates will vary anywhere from $25 to several hundred dollars an hour, depending on the lawyer, the demand for his time, his knowledge, and success in his field. Usually, the hourly rate for lawyers who serve the public will be $35 to $70 an hour. Young lawyers may charge less; lawyers with widely recognized proficiency may charge much more.

The important thing to you is how much the lawyer can accomplish for you in an hour. An efficient lawyer works rapidly. Consider the importance of the legal work involved. A $60-an-hour lawyer who knows what he is doing may do more for you in an hour with more satisfying results than a $25-an-hour lawyer can accomplish in several hours.

Per Diem Rate

A per diem rate is a charge for a day of the lawyer's time. Often, if a lawyer has to go into court, regardless of how many hours he has to stay there, he may charge for the day (per diem). Even if he is in court for only a few hours, the appearance may disrupt his schedule of interviews, and his work on other cases. The charge can vary from a couple of hundred to a thousand dollars, depending on the price of your legal talent and the circumstances. It is important to you to find out what your lawyer will charge and to get his schedule of charges.

Appearance Fees

Often lawyers going into court, even though they are expected to be there for only a short period, charge appearance fees, which can vary anywhere from $25 to several hundred dollars.

Adjustments for Results

When a lawyer undertakes a very complicated matter, if the results are either not good or the time required was more than anticipated, he may consider the results and bill you for only a part of his time. Likewise, on occasions when he gets an unusually good result with a small expenditure of time, he may be justified in increasing his fee.

When You Need a Lawyer Outside Your Locality

22

Perhaps while you are in a distant state, you are injured in an accident under circumstances such that you believe someone owes you money for your injuries. You need a lawyer to advise you on the local law and, perhaps, to represent you. Or suppose you are in business; you shipped merchandise to a store in a distant state, and you have not been paid. You need a lawyer to collect for the merchandise.

HOW TO SELECT COUNSEL OUTSIDE YOUR AREA

The best place to start is with your local lawyer. Go to see him. He has available to him some —and through his law library perhaps all—of the various law lists. Law lists are published directories of lawyers that frequently include meaningful information about their qualifications. These directories enable your lawyer to assist you to make an intelligent choice of counsel in the distant state.

If you have a claim for personal injuries and your medical treatment has taken place mostly in the area where you live, your local lawyer is an indispensable part of your legal team. He can best arrange for counsel to work with him in the area where the accident occurred and in which suit may have to be filed.

You can, if you wish, consult various law lists and make your own selection from them. Many of these law lists may be available in your local library.

The following paragraphs discuss the various law lists available. We have included addresses, should you wish to order a copy for your own use. Some lists are available only to lawyers. Some of these directories can be important to you in your business. For example, to assist you in collecting for merchandise not paid for, there are available no fewer than twelve law lists.

Lawyer's Register by Specialties and Fields of Law, 5325 Naiman Parkway, Solon, Ohio 44139. Phone: (216)248–0135. This is a national directory of the legal profession, categorized by legal specialties, which also includes a comprehensive directory of corporate counsel. By corporate counsel is meant lawyers who serve in the law departments of corporations. For many of the lawyers listed, meaningful biographical information is included. The register identifies those lawyers who are members of the Lawyer to Lawyer Consultation Panel. *The Lawyers Register by Specialties and Fields of Law* is the only directory for use by both the public and the profession that classifies lawyers by specialties and fields of law.

The Lawyer to Lawyer Consultation Panel Directory, 5325 Naiman Parkway, Solon, Ohio 44139. Phone: (216)248–0135. The Lawyer to Lawyer Consultation Panel is a national panel of lawyers who have been selected to counsel other lawyers in the various fields of law. Classification is by fields of law, and meaningful information is included about the listed lawyers. The standards for selection of lawyers for invitation to sit on the Panel include one or more of the following: certification as a specialist by the proper state authority, legal authorship, participation in legal seminars, teaching in accredited law schools, experience with government agencies or bureaus, leadership on substantive bar committees, and concentration of practice in one or a few related fields of law. Obviously, this is a directory of lawyer's lawyers. It is available only to lawyers. However, your lawyer can use it to make selection of local counsel. If your legal matter is very important to you, you will wish to retain a lawyer who is on the Panel. Panel members are listed and so identified in the *Lawyer's Register by Specialties and Fields of Law.* You will find it worthwhile to keep this in mind in referring to the *Register.*

Martindale-Hubbell Law Directory, One Prospect Street, Summit, New Jersey 07901. The most comprehensive and perhaps oldest law list is the *Martindale-Hubbell Law Directory.* It is a general legal directory. In the alphabetical section it lists alphabetically, by locality, the names, firm membership, addresses, phone numbers, age, law school, of all lawyers who are believed to be in the practice of law, privately, with a corporation, or with the government. The second part of each volume is the biographical section. In this section, lawyers and law firms who have a legal ability rating of "a" or "b" may purchase space to list their firm names and their lawyer personnel, again alphabetically by location, including biographical information. *Martindale-Hubbell* consists of seven large volumes; the seventh contains digests of the laws of the various states, Canada, and foreign countries. It also includes information on the various courts, the Uniform Commercial and Probate Code, plus other information.

Martindale-Hubbell rates the legal ability of some lawyers. Its rating system is quite controversial and, in many instances, its ratings are misleading. Many lawyers with outstanding national and even international reputations may either be given low ratings or none at all. The reason is the system of rating used. The ratings are based upon information from lawyers (who are already rated) and judges in the area where the lawyer practices. If the local lawyers do not like another lawyer, or are concerned with possible competition, they may rate him poorly. On the other hand, a lawyer who has been with a large firm that has an "a" rating may be discharged from the firm because of incompetency. Inasmuch as he has been with a firm that carries an "a" rating, he will most likely automatically get an "a" rating.

Martindale-Hubbell states, "Absence of rating characters

should not be construed as unfavorable as we do not undertake to publish ratings for all lawyers. Some have requested not to have any rating published while for others a definitive file has not been developed because of the relatively few years the lawyer has practiced, the size of the bar, or for other reasons unrelated to the individual's professional competence." Ten years admission to the bar is the minimum required for the legal ability rating of "a" (very high), five years for "b," and three years for "c" (fair).

General Law Lists

American Bank Attorneys
   Capron Publishing Corporation
   P.O. Box 387
   Wellesley Hills, Massachusetts 02181

The American Bar, The Canadian Bar,
The International Bar
   Reginald Bishop Forster & Associates
   121 West Franklin
   Minneapolis, Minnesota 55404

The Attorneys' Register
   The Attorneys' Register Publishing Co., Inc.
   636 Equitable Building
   Baltimore, Maryland 21202

The Bar Register
   The Bar Register Company, Inc.
   One Prospect Street
   Summit, New Jersey 07901

Campbell's List
   Campbell's List, Inc.
   Campbell Building
   Maitland, Florida 32751

The Lawyer's List
   The Law List Publishing Company, Inc.
   740 South Fulton Avenue
   Mount Vernon, New York 10550

List of Lawyers for Motorists
Automobile Legal Association
888 Worcester Street
Wellesley, Massachusetts 02181

Markham's Negligence Counsel
Markham Publishing Corporation
219 Atlantic Street
Stamford, Connecticut 06901

Motor Club of America Law List for Motorists
Motor Club of America
484 Central Avenue
Newark, New Jersey 07107

Russell Law List
Russell Law List
P.O. Box 1067
365 Fifth Avenue
Naples, Florida 33940

Transportation and Products Legal Directory
Transportation and Products
Legal Directory
Room 202
31 East Fifth Avenue
Gary, Indiana 46402

The United States Bar Directory
Attorneys' National Clearing House Co.
10297 Scarborough Road
Minneapolis, Minnesota 55437

The United States Lawyers Reference Directory
Legal Directories Publishing Co., Inc.
Suite 201
1314 Westwood Boulevard
Los Angeles, California 90024

Commercial Register

Birk's—Register of Commercial Attorneys
Attorneys' National Clearing House Co.

10297 Scarborough Road
Minneapolis, Minnesota 55437

Commercial Law Lists

Commercial lists are used principally by attorneys and others seeking to make collections.

American Lawyers Quarterly
The American Lawyers Company
Suite 1417, The East Ohio Building
Cleveland, Ohio 44114

The B. A. Law List
The B. A. Law List Co., Inc.
Suite 1000, Straus Building
238 West Wisconsin Avenue
Milwaukee, Wisconsin 53202

The Clearing House Quarterly
Attorneys' National Clearing House
10297 Scarborough Road
Minneapolis, Minnesota 55437

The Columbia List
Columbia Directory Company, Inc.
150 Broadway
New York, New York 10038

The Commercial Bar
Commercial Publishing Co., Inc.
740 South Fulton Avenue
Mount Vernon, New York 10550

The C-R-C Attorney Directory
The C-R-C Law List Company, Inc.
401 Broadway
New York, New York 10013

Forwarders List of Attorneys
Forwarders List Company, Inc.
636 Equitable Building
Baltimore, Maryland 21202

The General Bar
   The General Bar, Inc.
   The Bar Building
   36 West 44th Street
   New York, New York 10036

The International Lawyers
   International Lawyers Co., Inc.
   114 East 28th Street
   New York, New York 10016

The National List
   The National List, Inc.
   P.O. Box 401
   Yorktown Heights, New York 10598

Rand McNally List of Bank Recommended Attorneys
   Rand McNally & Company
   Bank Publications Division
   P.O. Box 7600
   Chicago, Illinois 60680

Wright-Holmes Law List
   S & H Publishers, Inc.
   485 Fifth Avenue
   New York, New York 10017

Probate Law Lists

The Probate Counsel
   Probate Counsel, Inc.
   Suite 510-C
   3033 North Central Avenue
   Phoenix, Arizona 85012

Insurance Law Lists

Best's Recommended Insurance Attorneys
   A. M. Best Co., Inc.
   Ambest Road
   Oldwick, New Jersey 08858

Hine's Insurance Counsel
Hine's Legal Directory, Inc.
P.O. Box 71
443 Duane Street
Glen Ellyn, Illinois 60137

The Insurance Bar
The Bar List Publishing Company
Willow Hill Executive Center
Northfield, Illinois 60093

Underwriters List of Trial Counsel
The Underwriters List Publishing Co., Inc.
22 East Twelfth Street
Cincinnati, Ohio 45210

State and Regional Directories

Alabama Legal Directory

Arkansas, Louisiana and *Mississippi Legal Directory*

California Legal Directory (with Arizona, Hawaii and Nevada Sections)

Florida Legal Directory

Georgia Legal Directory

Illinois Legal Directory

Indiana Legal Directory

Iowa Legal Directory

Kansas Legal Directory

Kentucky Legal Directory

Minnesota, Nebraska, North and *South Dakota Legal Directory*

Missouri Legal Directory

Mountain States Legal Directory (States of Colorado, Idaho, Montana, New Mexico, Utah and Wyoming)

New England Legal Directory (States of Connecticut, Maine, Massachusetts, New Hampshire, Rhode Island, and Vermont)

New York Legal Directory

North Carolina Legal Directory

Ohio Legal Directory
Oklahoma Legal Directory
Oregon and *Washington Legal Directory* (with Alaska Section)
Pennsylvania Legal Directory
South Carolina Legal Directory
Tennessee Legal Directory
Texas Legal Directory
Virginias, Maryland, Delaware and *District of Columbia Legal Directory*
Wisconsin Legal Directory
Legal Directories Publishing Co., Inc.
Suite 201
1314 Westwood Blvd.
Los Angeles, California 90024

Foreign Law Lists

Canadian Law Lists
Canada Law Book Company Limited
80 Cowdray Court
Agincourt, Ontario, Canada

The International Law List
L. Corper-Mordaunt & Company
London, W. C. 2, England

Kime's International Law Directory
Kime's International Law Directory, Ltd.
170 Sloane Street
London, SW1X 9QG, England

Obligations and
Responsibilities:
The Ethical Code

23

The legal profession has certain obligations to the public, just as individual lawyers have certain obligations to their clients. A lawyer who is admitted to practice in the state is bound to conduct himself by a very strict code of ethics. He *must* follow its Code of Professional Responsibility or face severe penalties imposed by the state lawyer authority, often the supreme court of that state.

The American Bar Association has published recommended *canons* or rules of conduct for members of the profession. These have no direct application to the individual lawyer. Each state adopts its own code that the lawyers admitted to practice in that state must abide by. It may follow the ABA draft or it may adopt a modified version.

In 1969 the rules were updated into the Code of Professional Responsibility. This code spells out the obligations of a lawyer to his clients (that is, the public) and to the legal profession, members of the bar, and the courts. The American Bar Association recognizes that as times change, so must the obligations of lawyers. A committee is presently studying possible changes for submission to the bar, some of which have already been submitted for adoption—particularly regarding lawyer advertising.

The organized bar recognizes that there are some lawyers who may not conduct themselves in the best interests of their clients or who may even be guilty of unethical or even dishonest conduct. To discourage and prevent unethical conduct and to control it, the state licensing authorities—usually the supreme court of the state—may suspend or remove (disbar) the lawyer from the practice of law. Most suspensions and disbarments are for the protection of the public and are of lawyers who have violated their obligations to the public.

When a lawyer who has served you has violated any of the Code's provisions to your detriment, the Code provides you with the means to redress the financial loss that may have occurred as a result. It does this in three ways. (1) The bar association can bring pressure upon the violating lawyer, who may repay you. (2) If he does not, the stage may be set for making a successful claim against him for malpractice. If he has an insurance carrier, the carrier will usually take care of the obligation, provided it is a case of malpractice. It is for this reason that the provisions of the Code of Professional Responsibility are important to you. (3) If you are not reimbursed by the lawyer (because he does not have sufficient funds) or by his insurance carrier, many bar associations have a client security fund. This may be used to reimburse you when the lawyer has been guilty of dishonesty and, in some areas, unethical or illegal conduct, provided sufficient funds are available.

The ethical obligations of lawyers are set forth in very technical language, which is hard for the layman to understand. The final draft of the Code of Professional Responsibility is 125 pages long. In addition there are many pages of opinions, formal and informal, by the American Bar Association's Standing Committee on Ethics and Professional Responsibility; many more opinions issued by similar committees of the various local and state associations; and many changes and interpretations issued by the courts.

We will outline here only those portions of the Code that should be of interest to you, and we will make no attempt to review the entire Code of Professional Responsibility and the many interpretations. Rather, we will summarize the canons of compelling interest to you and then try to translate each into common language where we feel it is necessary.

Canon 1: "A lawyer should assist in maintaining the integrity and competence of the legal profession." In plain language this means that each lawyer has a solemn duty to keep the legal profession honest and competent, beginning with himself. Under this canon a lawyer is honor-bound to be ethical and skillful in the practice of his profession.

Under our system of laws every person is entitled to legal representation. Lawyers as a group have the obligation to keep their professional standards high and to improve the competence of lawyers as a whole. Everyone in our society should be able to secure an independent lawyer who is competent (knows what he is doing and does it well).

Canon 2: "A lawyer should assist the legal profession in fulfilling its duty to make legal counsel available." A lawyer should make himself available to the public. He should provide information about himself that will help people to select him for legal services in his particular field of law. In this way he is assisting the profession in its duty to make legal counsel available. Under this canon, "advertising" of legal services in some way is part of a lawyer's professional responsibility.

Certainly education of the public is necessary. Laymen must be informed so that they can recognize their legal problems and appreciate the importance of seeking assistance. Something should be done to help the public select suitable legal counsel. (This book is the first of its kind to make such an attempt.)

To assist in making legal services fully available and to provide a process of intelligent selection, public information programs by the bar and advertising by lawyers may be necessary. A lawyer's listing in a reputable law list or legal directory giving biographic and other informative data has long been authorized by the canons of the bar association. This is a kind of advertising, but it is not readily available to laymen except for a few. The *Lawyer's Register By Specialties and Fields of Law* is among the few professional directories available to the public.

The prohibition by lawyers against lawyer advertising was abrogated by the United States Supreme Court in *Bates v. State Bar of Arizona.* Essentially this decision rendered by the Supreme Court was that without advertising the public does not have available sufficient information about lawyers to make intelligent choices to meet their specific needs. This, of course, has thrown the legal profession into turmoil. Generations of lawyers have been taught that advertising is immoral. Now they must cope with the fact that some kind of public information is necessary. The result is that the younger lawyers, being more adaptable, are tending to avail themselves of advertising.

Canon 3: "A lawyer should assist in preventing the unauthorized practice of law." Only a trained and competent lawyer should be allowed to represent a person with a legal problem. This is for your protection. Would you wish to be represented by an untrained person who has no credentials as a lawyer? Would you wish to be represented by a disbarred lawyer, who was kicked out of the profession because of dishonesty or moral turpitude? Lawyers police their profession to make sure that legal representation is ethical, responsible, and competent.

Canon 4: "A lawyer should preserve the confidences and secrets of his client." Under the code of ethics your lawyer must keep your secrets. What you tell your lawyer is confidential, and he is honor-bound to preserve your confidence and secrets. A client must feel free to discuss whatever he wishes with his lawyer. A lawyer must be equally free to ask questions and obtain information beyond that volunteered by his client.

A lawyer should be fully informed of all the facts in the matter he is handling for the client to obtain the full advantages of our legal system. It is for the lawyer to exercise his independent professional judgment to separate the the relevant and the important facts from the irrelevant and unimportant ones. Confidential handling, the ethical obligation of your lawyer to hold your secrets inviolate, is essential to proper legal representation. And it encourages persons who need a lawyer to seek legal assistance early.

Canon 5: "A lawyer should exercise independent professional judgment on behalf of the client." Your lawyer should work for you and for your best interests only, regardless of his personal interests. Your lawyer should, first of all, give you loyalty. He exercises his professional judgment within the bounds of the law solely for your benefit. He is ethically bound to serve you, regardless of compromising influences, desires of third persons, and personal interests.

Canon 6: "Your lawyer has to know his job [be competent] and do a good job for you, or hire [associate with] a lawyer who can do the job competently." Under this canon a lawyer has to decide whether he is competent in the matter before he accepts your case. Because of the complexities of law today, no lawyer can be competent and up to date in all 158 fields of law. Competent representation is vital to the success of your legal matter. Your lawyer should strive to become proficient in his practice and remain proficient in changing conditions. He should accept employment only in matters that he is competent to handle, or expects to become competent to handle.

A lawyer is aided to attain and maintain competence by keeping abreast of current legal literature and developments, participating in continuing legal education programs, concentrating in particular areas of the law, and by utilizing other available means. He has the additional ethical obligation to assist in improving the legal profession, and he may do so by participating in bar activities intended to advance the quality and standards of members of the profession. Of particular importance is the careful training of his younger associates and providing of sound guidance to all lawyers who consult him. In short, a lawyer should strive at all levels to help the legal profession advance the highest possible standards of integrity and competence and to meet those standards himself.

Although the licensing of a lawyer is evidence that he has met the standards prevailing for admission to the bar, a lawyer generally should not accept employment in any area of law in which he is not qualified. However, he may accept such employment in good faith if he expects to become qualified through study and investigation, as long as such preparation will not result in unreasonable delay or expense to his client. Proper preparation and representation in a legal matter may require the lawyer to secure assistance, to "associate" with professionals in other disciplines. A lawyer offered employment in a matter in which he is not and does not expect to become qualified should either decline the employment or, with the consent of his client, accept the employment and associate with a lawyer who is competent in the matter.

Having undertaken representation, a lawyer should use proper care to safeguard the interests of his client. If a lawyer has accepted employment in a matter beyond his competence but in which he expects to become competent, he should diligently undertake the work and study necessary to qualify himself. In addition requiring him to be qualified to handle a particular matter, his obligation to his client requires him to prepare adequately for and give appropriate attention to his legal work. He must not neglect a legal matter entrusted to him. Violation can result in disciplinary action.

Canon 7: "A lawyer should represent a client zealously within the bounds of the law." Your lawyer should fight for your rights and work hard and tirelessly for you. The duty of a lawyer, both to his client and to the legal system, is to represent his client zealously within the bounds of the law, which include Disciplinary Rules and enforceable professional regulations. The professional responsibility of a lawyer derives from his membership in a profession that has the duty to assist members of the public to secure and protect available legal rights and benefits. In our government of laws and not of men, each member of our society is entitled to have his conduct judged and regulated in accordance with the law; to seek any lawful objective through legally permissible means; and to present for adjudication any lawful claim, issue, or defense.

Canon 8: "A lawyer should assist in improving the legal system." Changes in human affairs and imperfections in human institutions require changes in our legal system; therefore, constant efforts must be made by lawyers to maintain and improve our legal system. This system should function in a manner that commands public respect and fosters the use of legal remedies to achieve redress of grievances. By reason of education and experience, lawyers are especially qualified to recognize deficiencies in the legal system and to initiate corrective measures therein. Thus they should participate in proposing and supporting legislation and programs to improve the system, without regard to the general interests or desires of clients or former clients.

Canon 9: "A lawyer should avoid even the appearance of

professional impropriety.'' Continuation of the American concept that we are to be governed by rules of law requires that the people have faith that justice can be obtained through our legal system. A lawyer should promote public confidence in our system and in the legal profession.

Public confidence in law and lawyers may be eroded by irresponsible or improper conduct of a lawyer. On occasion, ethical conduct of a lawyer may appear to laymen to be unethical. To avoid misunderstandings and, hence, to maintain confidence, a lawyer should fully and promptly inform his client of material developments in the matters being handled for the client. While a lawyer should guard against otherwise proper conduct that has a tendency to diminish public confidence in the legal system or in the legal profession, his duty to clients or to the public should never be subordinated merely because the full discharge of his obligation may be misunderstood or may tend to subject him or the legal profession to criticism. When explicit ethical guidance does not exist, a lawyer should determine his conduct by acting in a manner that promotes public confidence in the integrity and efficiency of the legal system and the legal profession.

THE CODE OF ETHICS PROTECTS YOU

If you believe that the lawyer representing you has been guilty of malpractice or dishonesty, the following chapter contains information about what you can do about it and how you can go about getting redress. However, we should emphasize here that *it is unwise for to you to make an unfounded claim against a lawyer.* Accusations without foundation will not only put him and you to unnecessary expense in terms of money and time, but it may ruin the lawyer's reputation without reason. But what should be the most important deterrent—to you—is that word of unmeritorious complaints tends to get around the profession. This means that in the future, if you have a problem requiring a lawyer's assistance, you will find it very difficult to secure competent legal service. Most lawyers will tend to shy away from representing you.

YOUR LAWYER CAN'T GUARANTEE RESULTS

One thing should be made clear to you. *A lawyer cannot guarantee that he will always secure a favorable result for you.* This is particularly true in a court action. Obviously, both sides of a case believe that their positions have merit. You may believe that your position has merit and the other position has none. What you must understand is that the opposing party may feel the same way. The only requirement is that your lawyer represent you competently. Two lawyers may disagree as to exactly how this should be done, but this does not indicate that either is wrong. The lawyer representing you is guilty of incompetence *only* if he has not exercised the skills that any lawyer in a similar situation should have possessed and exercised. Adequate knowledge and skill are the bases for competence.

Bar Associations Can Help You

24

Misunderstandings sometimes arise between lawyers and clients simply because of lack of communication. Sometimes a real problem does arise in which you can be assisted by a local bar association; for example, a fee dispute. Bar associations are set up to help you when you need help because of a problem with your lawyer. We will explore what the bar does to assist the public to obtain better legal service.

BAR ASSOCIATIONS
AND LEGAL SOCIETIES—HOW THEY CAN HELP

The "bar" is the legal profession as a whole. "Bar Associations" are organizations within the bar, groups of lawyers joining together generally for the advancement of the profession and to serve the public better.

A bar association may help you select a lawyer. It may be able to furnish you with information about some lawyers and

140

may be able to inform you about disciplinary proceedings against a lawyer.

The bar association also serves as a control over its members, initiating disciplinary proceedings against those members who violate the code of ethics. Disciplinary action on the part of the bar association against a member is a very serious thing to a lawyer, and such discipline can damage a lawyer's career and can result in disbarment.

Bar associations therefore protect and serve the public to help assure legal competence, ethical conduct, and the enforcement of professional standards in legal services.

LOCAL AND STATE BAR ASSOCIATIONS

Bar associations are local, state, and national. Lawyers of a large city will often have a bar association, and sometimes more than one. If there is more than one, the reason is often that one local bar association tends to be dominated by lawyers from large firms. The second bar association may consist of lawyers who represent less substantial interests and who have formed their own group so that they can be properly represented. Special nationality groups and religious groups may form their own associations. Thus we may have bar associations of black lawyers, Catholic lawyers, and lawyers who are veterans. In less populous areas the bar association may be organized on a county basis, and sometimes there may be only one bar association for several counties.

The next level is the *state bar association.*

In some states the membership is *voluntary.* This means that a lawyer can belong or not belong, as he wishes. In other states, membership is *compulsory.* A lawyer who is not a member of the state bar association is not permitted to practice in that state. Generally, state bar associations are more concerned with legal practice on a statewide basis rather than with local legal practice —the specific problems that may be encountered within a locality. Inasmuch as the membership is much larger than that of local bar associations, state association committees often offer greater diversity and concern themselves with a greater range of legal problems. State bar associations often make recommendations to state legislatures for needed changes in the law. This is a very important function of a state bar association.

NATIONAL BAR ASSOCIATIONS

The *American Bar Association* (ABA) is one of the largest professional organizations in the world. It has 235,000 members out of a profession of 450,000. (Many of these lawyers are not actively engaged in the practice of law. Some work in legal capacities for governments—local, state, and national—others work in legal departments of corporations.) The ABA considers problems of people and laws on a national basis.

The ABA's greater facilities enable it to consider problems on all levels and thus often to influence the actions later taken by the state and local bar associations.

The policymaking body of the ABA is the House of Delegates. Local and state bar associations and the ABA sections are represented in the House of Delegates. It also has members elected at large from the membership.

The ABA itself is a working organization with a multitude of committees and publications. Some of the standing committees are: Admiralty and Maritime Law, Aeronautical Law, Clients' Security Fund, Continuing Education of the Bar, Customs Law, Environmental Law, Ethics and Professional Responsibility, Federal Judiciary, Judicial Section, Tenure and Compensation, Lawyer Referral Service, Lawyers in the Armed Forces, Lawyers' Title Guaranty Funds, Legal Aid and Indigent Defendants, Legal Assistants, Legal Drafting, Legislation, Membership, Military Law.

Some of the special committees and commissions are: National Conference Groups, Professional Career Development, Professional Discipline, Implementation of Specialization, Standards and Codes, Unauthorized Practice of the Law, World Order under Law, Administration of Criminal Justice, Automobile Insurance Legislation, Code of Ethics for Commercial Arbitrators, Commission on Correctional Facilities and Services, Delivery of Legal Services, Election Reform, Energy Law,

Committee to Study Federal Law Enforcement Agencies, Federal Limitations on Attorneys' Fees, Housing and Urban Development Law, Commission on Law and Economy, Law Book Publishing Practices, Lawyers in Government, Lawyers' Professional Liability, Legal Assistance for Military Personnel, Committee for a Study of Legal Education, Committee to Survey Legal Needs, Consortium on Legal Services and the Public, Commission on Medical Professional Liability, Commission on Mentally Disabled, On the Resolution of Minor Disputes, Commission on a National Institute of Justice, Prepaid Legal Services, Public Interest Practice, Residential Real Estate Transactions, Retirement Benefits Legislation, Commission on Standards of Judicial Administration, Student Loan Fund, Youth Education for Citizenship.

In addition, the ABA is divided into sections, each one on a specialty basis. They are semiautonomous and elect their own chairmen and section councils. Lawyers who belong to the ABA usually also belong to one or more sections that reflect the kind of practice that they have. They are: Administrative Law; Antitrust Law; Bar Activities; Corporation, Banking, and Business Law; Criminal Justice; Economics of Law Practice; Family Law; General Practice; Individual Rights and Responsibilities; Insurance, Negligence and Compensation Law; International Law; Labor Relations Law; Legal Education and Admissions to the Bar; Litigation; Local Government Law; Natural Resources Law; Patent, Trademark and Copyright Law; Public Contract Law; Public Utility Law; Real Property; Probate and Trust Law; Science and Technology; Taxation; Young Lawyers; Judicial Administration Division; and Law Student Division.

Each section, in turn, has numerous committees. For example, the Family Law section has the following committees, each of which strives to improve the law, lawyers' knowledge, and service to the public: Adoption, Alimony, Maintenance and Support, Bill of Rights for Children, Custody, Divorce Law and Procedures, Education for Parenthood, Ethics in the Family and in Family Law, Family Courts and Family Law Judges, Subcommittee of Model Family Court Act, Family Law Specialization and Certification, Mediation and Arbitration, Mental

Retardation Law and Ethics, Paternity and Illegitimacy, The Practicing Lawyer, Rights of the Family and its Members, Research, Scope, Supervision and Evaluation of Committees, Law and Psychiatry (Liaison with American Psychiatric Association), Liaison with Commissioners on Uniform State Laws, Liaison with Law Student Division, Liaison with Section of Criminal Justice, Liaison with Section of Individual Rights and Responsibilities, Liaison with Section of International Law, Liaison with Section of Taxation, Liaison with Young Lawyers Section, International Legal Exchange Program, Public Information, Publications, Family Legal Assistance for Service Personnel, The Family of Tomorrow (Revitalization of the Family), Federal Legislation and the Family, Genetic Counseling in the Family and the Law, Interstate and International Support, Juvenile Justice (Joint with Section of Criminal Justice and Judicial Administration Division), Juvenile Law and Procedure, Law and Family Planning, Legal Problems of the Aging, Marriage and Family Counseling and Conciliation, and Marriage Law.

A great deal of the activity of the ABA and its sections is on *how to serve the public better or more effectively.* Considerable activity is devoted to protecting the rights of the public. In the past the ABA has been quite conservative; but today, with almost 50% of its membership consisting of lawyers under 35 years of age, it generally is more liberal in its view than most state and local bar associations and advocates changes in the profession to a far greater extent. Young lawyers, like other young people, are sensitive to the changing needs of society. They are quite effective in advocating and securing needed changes both within the bar and outside it.

Lawyers who practice specialties often have their own bar associations on a national basis. Thus we have the *Federal Bar Association,* which consists generally of lawyers whose practice deals with or has dealt with work for the federal government. Then we have associations of lawyers who do specialized work, such as *Federation of Insurance Counsel* (insurance company defense), *American Trial Lawyers* (lawyers who represent injured parties in their claims against insurance companies), *National College of Criminal Defense Lawyers and Public Defenders,* to mention only a few.

WHAT TO DO IF YOU HAVE A COMPLAINT

If you think you have a complaint against a local lawyer, you should first take up the problem with your local bar association. The local bar association usually has a grievance committee—lawyers who will sympathetically handle your complaint. More often than not a complaint is a result of a misunderstanding, and the grievance committee will assist in getting the matter cleared up. If you think you have been defrauded (a very rare occurrence), it will assist you to get redress from a "client security fund." It will also take appropriate action to discipline or disbar the lawyer. More often the dispute may concern the fee, and the committee will help resolve the matter. If you and the lawyer agree, some bar associations will arrange for the fee dispute to be resolved through binding arbitration.

The local bar can often also assist you in your selection of a lawyer. Some local and state bar associations have lawyer referral plans. Some are organized along specialty lines and will refer you to a lawyer who practices in the field in which your problem falls. Others simply refer you to the next lawyer on their list, regardless of the nature of his practice and your problem. If you wish to use a referral plan, request details about a lawyer's qualifications. He may not be the lawyer you need.

HOW THE BAR PROTECTS YOU

Lawyers as a class are generally honorable and ethical in their conduct. They have to be if they wish to maintain their good standing in the profession. Unfortunately, the public is often given the wrong impression. In the cases of the few lawyers who do go wrong, the public is given the impression by the press that wrongdoing on the part of lawyers is widespread. A lawyer's reputation is the stock in trade of his career. If a lawyer engages in dishonest or unethical conduct, the profession often deals swift, harsh judgment, and such a lawyer may be suspended or disbarred. Unfortunately, this is not always the case. Some states are lax in disciplining lawyers. Generally, court rules require that discipline be handled privately by the bar. The lawyer who has committed offenses punishable by disbarment is asked to resign and is not allowed to practice law thereafter. The public generally doesn't realize that some lawyers who claim that they are tired of practicing law and, therefore, are engaged in some other vocation may have been asked to resign from the bar because of their lack of ethics or honesty.

A person has to be of good character to be admitted to a law school. Most bar committees check out the character of the applicant before he is admitted to the bar. If a lawyer is involved in any activity that casts aspersions on his honesty, or if he is guilty of moral turpitude, most areas will not permit him to be licensed or to practice law.

Because public announcement is rarely made, the public does not know that the bar does a reasonably good job of policing the character and ethics of its members. When a lawyer does go bad, the excessive use of alcohol is frequently involved. For this reason, if you know or suspect that a lawyer is a heavy drinker, avoid engaging him. Generally, *competency* of a lawyer is your main problem. Lawyers may range from excellent to poor in the practice of their profession. Fortunately for the public, most (but not all), lawyers can handle most matters reasonably well.

What To Do
If You're Dissatisfied
With Your Lawyer

25

You are entitled to discharge your present lawyer at any time that you wish. However, you owe him for the services that he has rendered prior to his discharge. This is true whether you hired him on a *time basis* or on a *contingent fee* basis. (A time basis means that you pay a fee for hours worked in your behalf. A contingent fee basis means that the lawyer takes his fee as a percentage of the amount recovered for you.)

Determining what you owe the lawyer retained by you on a contingent fee basis can sometimes be difficult. When you agreed to have the lawyer represent you on a contingent fee basis, you signed an agreement. The agreement provides for a percentage of the recovery to be paid to the lawyer from the amount coming to you either by way of settlement or by trial. If the lawyer has obtained an offer that he has recommended you accept but you refuse it, you owe him a fee based on the amount offered, according to the percentage in the contract you signed. If he has rendered services but has not reached the point where he has obtained an offer or what he considers to be a reasonable offer, you owe him for the reasonable value of the services that he has rendered you.

Until you pay him or make arrangements satisfactory to him for payment, he may have the right to keep the papers that he has in his file. These are his work product, and under the law of many states (but not all) he has a lien against these. Accordingly, you must either pay him or make arrangements with him concerning his fee, whether it be on the basis of reasonable value of his time or the amount that you owe on a contingent basis. Such arrangement can be communicated to the successor attorney (the new lawyer you wish to represent you) with instructions that the original lawyer's fee be protected out of settlement or verdict.

Generally, an attorney will not agree to succeed the original attorney unless you have been released by the original attorney and often only after you have made satisfactory arrangements for the original attorney's fee.

Even though you have not made satisfactory arrangements with the original attorney concerning his fee, *you are still entitled to legal representation.* However, if you do not make satisfactory arrangements concerning his fee with your original lawyer, you will find that very few competent lawyers will agree to represent you. The reason is a second lawyer may be concerned that you may likewise fail to take care of his fee. Another reason is that if your matter is on a contingent basis, the successor attorney may have a problem concerning the contract you made with your original attorney, and this may also impede settlement. The original attorney may have a claim against any settlement or verdict that even the insurance carrier of the defendant may have to honor. Accordingly, *it is best to make your arrangements with the original attorney, leaving yourself free to be able to obtain the best possible representation by a succeeding attorney.*

WHAT IF YOUR ATTORNEY WITHDRAWS?

Your attorney has the right to withdraw his representation of you.

He may wish to withdraw for various reasons: Lack of your cooperation may be a reason for withdrawal. Failure to honor the fee agreement is another good reason. Your attorney may withdraw for any reason that he believes appropriate. However, the Code of Professional Responsibility states, "A decision by a lawyer to withdraw should be made only on the basis of compelling circumstances, and in a matter pending before a tribunal, he must comply with the rules of the tribunal regarding withdrawal." It further goes on to state, "A lawyer should not withdraw without considering carefully and endeavoring to minimize the possible adverse affect on the rights of his client and the possibility of prejudice to his client as a result of his withdrawal."

The withdrawing lawyer must do everything possible to protect your welfare and give due notice of his withdrawal, including suggesting employment of other counsel and delivering to the client all papers and properties to which the client is entitled in cooperating with counsel subsequently employed. Further, the withdrawing lawyer must refund to you any compensation not earned during the employment.

WHEN A LAWYER MUST WITHDRAW FROM A CASE

A lawyer *must withdraw from representing you* before a tribunal (which includes, of course, a court) *if he knows* or if it is obvious *that you are bringing the legal action* or conducting the defense or asserting a position in litigation or otherwise having steps taken *merely for the purpose of harassing or maliciously injuring any person.*

He also *must withdraw* if it is obvious that his continued employment will result in a violation by him of a disciplinary rule. He also *must withdraw* if his mental or physical condition renders it unreasonably difficult for him to carry out his employment effectively and, of course, *he must withdraw if he is discharged by you.*

ASSOCIATING ANOTHER LAWYER

A lawyer cannot represent you when he is unable to render competent service to you. He may, with your permission, associate another lawyer with him who is competent. He cannot associate another lawyer without your permission.

REPRESENTING MULTIPLE CLIENTS
WITH DIFFERING INTERESTS

Your lawyer represents many clients, and there are times when your lawyer may be representing more than one client as a result of one legal situation. However, he is not permitted to represent in litigation or any other way multiple clients with differing interests. The reason is that he could not be fair to all the clients (of different interests) and under such circumstances should withdraw from representing those clients with whom he has differing interests.

If you have given your lawyer every opportunity to do his best work for you—and you have cooperated with him—and you are still not satisfied—get another lawyer!

Courts

26

If you have a problem that may entail the use of courts, it may help you to have a basic knowledge about them. It should be emphasized that courts from state to state vary in name and sometimes in nature. They vary as to the amount of money, the kinds of matters, and the geographic areas in which they have jurisdiction to decide legal disputes. But generally they tend to follow the same format.

LOCAL COURTS

If a city is of sufficient size, it will often have what is termed the *Municipal Court*. Sometimes this is merely a division of the court of general jurisdiction. Usually the jurisdiction of such court extends only to the confines of a municipality. It can generally handle most but not all matters that occur within the municipality, such as accidents or crimes. It often has a monetary limit—usually $5000 or $10,000. This is the largest amount that anyone using such a court can sue for. In criminal matters, it usually has jurisdiction of only minor crimes and traffic offenses. Some municipal courts "turn" or "bind" accused people over to a grand jury or to a court of unlimited jurisdiction. This is a preliminary hearing to determine if the person should be further charged with a crime. Municipal courts can also take jurisdiction of some events that occurred outside the municipality when the person being sued resides within the municipality.

In many localities the municipal court maintains what is often termed a *Small Claims Court*. This is a division set up to handle claims under a certain sum (often under $1000), claims of people against other people, and claims that do not necessitate the services of a lawyer. In fact, *many small claims courts prohibit representation of either side by a lawyer.* The reason is that small claims often do not involve enough money to permit the economical services of a lawyer.

In other areas, particularly rural counties, there may be what may be known as a *County Court*. We refer to a court that has limited jurisdiction (like the municipal court) and that has a limitation on the amount for which you can sue and the kind of cases the court can accept.

In many localities *Justice of Peace Courts* still exist. These are tending to disappear, since the reason for their existence is also tending to disappear. Generally, the Justice of the Peace is not a lawyer. The purpose of the Justice of the Peace is to give citizens of a small or isolated community a local "court" that is very limited in jurisdiction and usually confined to minor matters to assist local citizens to adjudicate their disputes.

COURTS OF GENERAL JURISDICTION

These courts also go under various names. In some areas they are called the *Court of Common Pleas*. In other areas they are called the *Superior Court* and in others they may be referred to as a *Supreme Court* (of course, when so named, they are not the court of last resort.) These courts can take jurisdiction of cases involving any amount or any legal matter, with the exception of cases that can only be adjudicated by federal courts (such as bankruptcy matters). However, although these are general jurisdiction courts, they cannot take jurisdiction where they do not have what is commonly referred to as "venue." Venue means the authority to act within the geographic area where the cause of action arose or where the defendant resides, has an office, or does substantial business. "A change of venue" means that the matter must go to a court in some other area or perhaps to a U.S. Federal Court.

MOTIONS FOR NEW TRIAL

If, after trial of a case, you believe the jury verdict or the court's judgment is wrong, the first step addressed to a trial court may be a "motion for new trial," a request for a *remittitur* (to reduce the amount of the verdict), an *additor* (to increase it), or "judgment (by the court) notwithstanding the verdict." In many courts, such motions must be in writing and contain a "brief" stating the legal reasons why the court should grant the motion. Some courts also require that such motions be argued in person by the lawyers involved.

COURTS OF APPEAL

Where you feel that you have not been accorded justice in a lower court, your lawyer may appeal to a *Court of Appeals*. Generally they will review the record (if the appeal is from a *Court of Record*—a court where the testimony of witnesses is preserved by some means) of what happened. This can be quite costly, particularly if it involves a trial that has taken many days. This often requires the court reporter's typing out a *transcript* of all of the proceedings. In some jurisdictions the testimony of witnesses and court rulings in a lower court is recorded electronically, sometimes with a tape recorder and other times with a videotape recorder. In some areas you can appeal using this means without reducing the testimony to writing. This, of course, expedites matters and makes appeal much easier, quicker, and much less expensive.

Some courts, such as Justice of Peace Courts, are not

courts of record. When you appeal from such a court, you have no record; accordingly, you may have to try the case again. You may also be limited as to what you can "appeal" about. Usually such appeals are to a court of general jurisdiction and not to a court of appeals. If you believe prejudicial error has been made in the court of general jurisdiction you can appeal again, this time to a court of appeals.

Your lawyer for the court of appeals prepares a brief wherein he calls the court's attention to the nature of the error, cites law cases that prove his point, and states why your case should be sent back for retrial or a different result should be awarded. The opposing side likewise has the opportunity of preparing an answering brief. Some courts of appeal will *permit* the parties to submit the matter on briefs, others will *require* it. Most will permit the attorneys to orally argue their case before the court of appeals. (Many courts of appeals will permit attorneys to forgo oral argument and submit the appeal on the briefs.) Members of a court of appeals may and often do avail themselves of the opportunity to ask questions of counsel, which may be important in making their determination.

The court of appeals then may reverse the matter and enter final judgment in favor of the complaining party, modify the judgment in some manner, or send the case back to the trial court for retrial.

A third and last layer of appeal is often called the *Supreme Court,* though in some jurisdictions it may go by another name. Generally, a supreme court does not have to accept the appeal. There must be good reason for acceptance. Accordingly, there is usually *a motion to appeal* (sometimes called by other names), which often is acted upon by the court after reading the briefs of both sides without benefit of oral argument. In some jurisdictions oral argument is permitted. If the court considers the case of great public interest or if it involves constitutional grounds that are set forth in the state laws or its constitution, it will allow the appeal.

Transcripts of the proceedings that occurred in the trial court then must be filed along with the decision and written opinion (if any) of the appellate court. In addition, the parties file briefs as to their positions. Again, the case may be submitted in brief form or argued orally. In some instances personal arguments are not permitted. The court then may dispose of the case in the same way as does an appellate court. That is, reverse the final judgment, modify it, or send it back to the trial court for retrial.

UNITED STATES (FEDERAL) COURTS

The courts at the lowest level of the federal court system are called *United States District Courts*. These usually encompass a district, which generally includes far more area than a single city except for very large cities. A single U.S. District Court frequently is made up of more than one court and more than one judge. Some of the judges may travel to other cities and actually hold court in these other cities. As part of a District Court we have the Bankruptcy Court with a Bankruptcy Judge. As the name implies, bankruptcy courts only consider bankruptcy matters.

The *United States Court of Claims* is a specialized court that considers suits against the United States, patent and copyright matters, and reviews decisions of the Indian Claims Commission. The *United States Customs Court* considers actions arising under tariff acts, while the *United States Court of Customs and Patent Appeals* reviews decisions of the U.S. Customs Court. The *United States Court of Military Appeals* considers appeals in court-martial convictions in the various military services. The *United States Tax Court* considers federal tax disputes. As in state courts, there are United States appellate courts similar in function to the appellate courts on state level.

The United States Supreme Court, like the supreme courts of the states, does not accept appeals as a matter of right but usually determines whether it wishes to accept the appeal. If it so wishes, the court will hear it. The United States Appellate and Supreme Courts usually only consider appeals from U.S. District Courts, Tax Courts, etc. However, on certain occasions they will review decisions of the various state supreme courts.

How to Save Money
On Legal Services

27

Now that you have read this book, you should be informed of the many ways in which you can save money on legal services. These have been mentioned throughout the book under various chapters pertaining to the employment of lawyers and to the legal system. The purpose of this chapter is to bring these suggestions together, clarify their use, and give additional suggestions so that you can obtain maximum savings in the employment of lawyers.

So that you will not overlook any moneysaving suggestions, the topics have been set up as a checklist questionnaire. To avoid duplication when a suggestion has been covered quite fully elsewhere in the book, the page numbers will be furnished. When a suggestion was not covered or not covered adequately, you will find additional information and examples.

1. *Is your problem really a legal matter?* If you have any question as to whether your problem is a legal matter, you may find it desirable to consult a lawyer.

2. *Do you think you handle this problem yourself without a lawyer?*

3. Can some other professional do the job for you as well at lower cost?

4. How important is this matter to you? Even if you determine that this is a matter that should be handled by a lawyer, you must ask yourself another question: Is it worth an attorney's fee and your time to pursue the matter? If it is not important enough, then it is better to forget about it.

Some people incur substantial fees to enforce or secure legal rights of little or no value. Some people pursue a legal matter because of "the principle." What is even worse, matters of principle or of inconsequential value often turn out to be very expensive in lawyer's time and not infrequently do more harm than good.

For example, suppose you hear that a neighbor has made a defamatory statement about you. You are angry and decide you want to sue the neighbor for slander. You rush to consult a lawyer. You ask the lawyer if he would handle this case on a contingent basis. He will most likely inform you that he does not handle cases of that kind on a contingent basis. He states that he wants $50 an hour along with a several-hundred-dollar retainer.

You are so angry that you wish to teach your neighbor a lesson. You quickly discover that cases of this sort are time-consuming for both you and your lawyer. After several refreshers of retainer to your lawyer, you may find that the rumor was not true or that it was exaggerated and that you have no case. Furthermore, you have alienated a neighbor who may have been friendly to you. Worse is the unfavorable publicity. Even if the statement about you had been true, few people knew of it before; now many know about it and some may believe it. Worse yet, you've taught no one a lesson except yourself, as you have incurred large attorney's fees unnecessarily.

Suppose you and your spouse fight all the time and you just can't get along. Finally you are sued for divorce. You know that the marriage is not working out and that nothing can be done to save it. But you're angry, so you see an attorney about contesting the divorce. After you have run up sizable attorney's fees (depending on how angry you are), you finally accept your lawyer's advice and withdraw contesting the divorce.

If you think that either of these are isolated occurrences, ask a lawyer who handles divorce cases. He will tell you that many divorces are contested but that very, very few remain contested through trial. Of course, some divorces are contested solely to obtain a bargaining position. Likewise, attorneys who handle neighborhood squabbles will tell you how needless and expensive they often are.

5. *When should you see a lawyer?* The answer is as soon as possible, once you have determined that you have a legal problem and that you should consult an attorney about it. Too often people procrastinate about seeing a lawyer and protecting their legal rights. Witnesses that could have assisted you to prove your rights may move to places unknown to you, may die, or their testimony may become otherwise unavailable. What might have been an inexpensive problem may require considerable services to locate witnesses and establish your rights. Furthermore, this can result in further cost to you by your losing legal rights. Most causes of action have statutes of limitations within which rights must be enforced. For example, in many jurisdictions if you are injured and believe you have a case, unless you do something about it in two years your right expires.

6. *Did you write a short summary of your problem before you called for an appointment?* If the amount of the consultation fee is important to you, be sure to ask the lawyer how much it is.

7. *Have you prepared for your first office visit?* Since most consultations are on a time basis, whatever you can do before your consultation to make it easier and quicker for the lawyer to give you advice will cut the amount of the consultation fee, if it is on a time basis.

8. *Did you ask your lawyer what his fee basis is?* If it's a contingent fee and you have a good case, he may quote you a lower percentage than he would otherwise. The reason: He may be concerned that you will leave to secure other counsel. For the same reason, if it's a matter to be handled on an hourly basis, he may quote you a smaller hourly rate than he might otherwise charge. Similarly, if your legal matter can be estimated, such as a name change, an uncontested divorce, or a deed, you may save money by asking what he charges in advance.

9. *Did you request an itemized bill?* If you have retained the attorney on an hourly basis and he has concluded the matter, be sure that he sends you an itemized bill stating what

he did and the amount of time involved. Having to itemize what he has done and the amount of time involved will often result in a smaller bill than would otherwise be rendered. Should any of the charges appear out of line, this can be called to his attention and may result in adjustment. For example, suppose he writes a simple letter and charges you for an hour of his time for it. On questioning, he may adjust that to a much lesser figure.

10. *What can you do to assist your lawyer in the handling of your case?* In many matters, you yourself can obtain needed evidence documents or information that the lawyer may need. For example, suppose you have had an accident and are consulting a lawyer to determine if you have a valid claim. He informs you that he cannot answer the question without first obtaining a police report. You would be smart to volunteer to obtain it.

11. *Do you make the mistake of telephoning and conferring with your lawyer unnecessarily?* Every time you call or see him you have incurred a charge. Furthermore, he may have to send his secretary for your file. He may have to call you back and you may be out. You then have to return his call—and you have incurred another charge.

12. *Do you raise unimportant points or object to inconsequential matters?* You ask your lawyer to draw an agreement for you. He complies with your request, but you object to certain phraseology. Your lawyer points out that the change you wish is unimportant. Nevertheless, you want it changed. You have unnecessarily raised the cost to you, as he now has to redictate that portion of the agreement. His secretary has to retype it. Since it may involve a whole page and sometimes several pages, it means that he may have to recheck several pages to be sure there is no mistake. If there is, he may have to have it retyped and rechecked again.

One of the most costly problems in handling agreements that involve other parties is that often both clients may object to inconsequential items. If you are submitted an agreement that your lawyer believes is in order and you object to an inconsequential item, you may raise the cost by far more than you realize. Your attorney has to call the opposing attorney concerning the change. The opposing attorney has to call his client and then has to call your attorney. Your attorney has to call you, and then he has to redraft the agreement.

13. *Are you truthful with your lawyer?* Some clients relate as facts stories that they *wish* were the facts. These may mislead their attorneys into believing that the clients have certain rights that they may not have. By the time attorneys find out the truth, they may have spent needless hours and expended needless money at the clients' expense, not to mention that the clients themselves may have spent many hours needlessly.

For example, a client consults an attorney who informs him that he has a questionable cause of action. The attorney explains why. The client then consults another attorney and *changes the facts* so that now it would appear that he *does* have a good cause of action. He may have fooled his attorney, but that does not change the facts, and this can be quite costly when discovered. Furthermore, the client may have turned a questionable case into one that he has less chance of winning.

Similar situations arise in business dealings because a client will avoid telling his lawyer unpleasant facts that are discovered later after costing the client needless legal fees.

14. *Did you select the lawyer who can competently handle your matter at the lowest cost?* If your legal matter is not very important, you may well consider hiring a young lawyer. He will, as previously indicated, work for less than an older lawyer. If you have a highly complex matter, you will find it both cheaper and productive of better results to consult a lawyer who concentrates his practice in the problem area.

If you will use lawyers judiciously and consult them as often and expeditiously as necessary, you will save yourself lots of legal costs over the years.

Index